SZEN ZONE

SZEN
ZONE

REACHING A STATE OF POSITIVE CHANGE

Gary D Szenderski

FingerTouch
Books

Dedication
This book is dedicated to all of the loyal readers and followers of the Book of Szen. Your support and encouragement has been a gift and has brought the Szen Zone to life. Thank you.

Introduction

My earlier book, The *Book of Szen*, is a compilation of stories written and shared over many years. The response was very positive and inspired and encouraged me to continue writing, and now, a few years later, the *SZEN ZONE* emerges. It contains lighthearted and positive narrative on life and its possibilities, with stories that cover the gamut from interesting to profound. The general overarching theme has been on *change* and all of the aspects of it - Creating, surviving, and managing change with the goal to recognize the power we have to become what we choose, both when we're feeling in control and how to mange when we're not in control.

In terms of how to go about reading this book, it is up to you. Open it anywhere and find a short story that may make your day or make you think. My own copy has dog-ears, post-it notes and sections highlighted and underlined. I find it useful to review key ideas that remind me that change is constant and so is life and that our perspective makes a difference in how all of it unfolds.

The SZEN ZONE focuses on identifying the lift-off point for creating positive change. Although everyone is different and it's a very individual and sometimes internalized process, the principles in this book can help you establish the context and right frame of mind to embrace and manage change. After many years of professionally helping individuals and companies navigate change, I've observed how some changes seem to take forever while unforeseen change can come right at you and in an instant move your world.

To that end, wherever you may find yourself at this moment, you will find an insight or example in this book to help you change course and take charge.

The files that they are drawn from will help guide you too. I've categorized them here:

Szenabling File – *Ideas and insights to spark motivation*
Szenippets – *The end point of each story*
Now & Szen – *Memories and perspective recast*
60 Word Szen Story – *Stories to introduce the topic*
Make Shift – *Time to take charge*

Szenippet: If I told you that change would be easy, you may not believe me. But if I said that it's possible, you would cast your doubt aside. Once we see "it", we can be "it."

An Excerpt from: *A Course in Creation*
We are not our resume'. Nor are we what we own or how we look or sound. We are not what others see when they look at us. We are not the title, or the paycheck, or the car or the

house. We are not without power. We are not weak or limited. "Where" we are does not define who we are.

What all of us are, is how we end this sentence: I am…"____." If we could take some time to consider how often we sabotage our day or our thinking by finishing that sentence with a debilitating premise such as I am sick or tired or poor or alone etc. we could turn the moments of doubt and discomfort into something different, and better. To say to ourselves: I am strong, rich, powerful, healthy, alive and in love etc. are viable options too.

Creation takes place when we change the sentence. By listening to our inner voice within we can begin contemplating a grander presence and a new day and life. Filling in the blanks with a dream actually begins the process of bringing the dream to life. The pronouncement of I am "___" is whatever we want to be, or feel called to be; it is the key to change, which is where we find the seeds to create.

"I am" triggers thoughts, actions and events that will confirm what we believe. We literally live up to our own declarations of self. Change the script and everything changes with it. It's a simple notion, and it works, and **I am** really happy that you let me share this with you. I hope you enjoy reading this book as much as I have writing it.

In every seed of change is the power to create something new. To leave what was, close a door and move toward a new, better version of ourselves.

Contents

Editor's Notes

Catherine Green, a colleague, friend and a gifted writer prepared short notes for me while editing this book that summarizes some of the stories like mini-previews. They appear at the beginning of each chapter.

Acknowledgments

The only reason that this book exists at all is because so many readers have confided that they have found a word, phrase or passage that has helped them realign their thinking and understanding of their ultimate potential.

To get to those words and insights takes a village filled with love and real smart people. These people pushed, prodded and cheered me to keep the message coming. They include all of the Book of Szen readers that asked for more, and those that added special insights, clarity and assistance to the process. This includes: Barry Kibrick host of Between the Lines on PBS provided incredible validation, and the desire to write more. Dirk Mynatt, for a clean cover design and concept that I think captures the spirit of SZEN ZONE. Sandie Sedgebeer a professional writer, editor and interviewer that in every way gets to the point. Her feedback added another dimension of authenticity. Jerry Walters, a great friend and mentor whose belief in me kept me grounded. Catherine Green, who edited with a joy and thoroughness that made it easier to read and in many ways more profound. My two sons: Maxwell and Adam, who chimed in with opinion and wit and spread the word to a new generation. And Jane. She was there for me throughout and brought love, encouragement and plenty of ideas.

CHAPTER 1

Boldly go

BE BRAVE, BE BOLD, BE YOUR BEST

*Overcoming obstacles, limiting ideas and anything
else that's holding you back in life.*

CHAPTER ONE EDITOR'S NOTES – A PREVIEW

IN LIFE

Self – Discovery, The Journey Within (go inside to figure out what you want to do with your life)

E Spot (clear away the old debris to tap into your energy source.)

The Key to Life (Buddy's homeless story)

Smoke Brake (it only takes one epiphany to give up a bad habit.)

Brand Aid (fixing or updating your personal brand)

Help is On the Way (ask for help, people will be happy to give it)

Attitude Rules (a positive attitude will drive you to success)

Rain of Fear (develop a glass half full attitude and don't let the rain get you down)

No Will, No Way (Be bold in the face of fear)

En Garde (living in the moment and being ready for everything, will give you the best chance for success)

Self-Discovery
The Journey Within
From the Make Shift File:

I'm a teacher and on the very first day of school I like to take a survey of the students and ask them what it is, exactly, that they want to accomplish not only in class, but also in life. The answers are as varied as the degree of certainty in the answers. Some people seem to know exactly whom they are and where they are going, and others are still searching for a vision and a goal that defines their life.

What we want to be when we grow up can be elusive for sure, and often our actions contradict our stated goals. The reason this happens is because our stated goals are not what we really want, but rather what others expect of us. The real, deeper and stronger dream inside can be buried by obligations, phobias and doubts. Sadly, after a while, we lose the clarity we need to let our real self emerge. We know we want more, but we're not sure what it is that we need. This leads to complacency, allowing us to compromise our greatest aspirations for lesser goals.

To be clear on what we want, we have to search inside. Only our internal compass can determine if we're on our true path. That compass is only activated when we know who we really are. The power of self-discovery starts the internal engine that puts our destiny into view and our journey into gear. And the only way to know if it's right is to question our feelings about ourselves. Here is a quick reference:

- We have to feel worthy of the dream
- We have to enjoy what we're dreaming
- We have to see the dream coming true

To know ourselves is to understand that what's swirling around in our sub-conscious are signs. It's appreciating that the identification and embracing of what's real and possible for us is only as good as what we recognize as true and believe within. It creates an inescapable calm and confidence and from there, anything is possible.

Szenippet: The key to getting what you want in life, is to really know what you want in life.

■ ■ ■

The E Spot

Everything everyone enjoys enters; evolves - eventually engaging each entity entirely. Easy? Exactly.

The e-spot is our own personal energy source. For some it's only a pilot light that maintains just enough oomph to get us through the day. While for others, it's an inferno ablaze with desire to achieve greatness. What controls the intensity of our own internal flame is always personal and filtered through our own unique perspective. Perspective is actually the fodder for flame and the catalyst for positive change.

Perspective to the e-spot is like oxygen to the fire. Perspective directs and frames choices, creates decisions and defines our dreams. When we feel engaged and energized, it's because our point of view is in alignment not only with the goal, but also with the means to get there. We somehow *know* we can do it. It's the e-spot telling us we have the fuel to make the trip.

If we need more fuel for our own personal trip, we can take a look at your own focal point and perspective. Usually only a tweak or two will open the energy valves. Sometimes it's getting rid of some part of the past that's clogging up our thinking, but more often it's not the elimination of a clog but the creation of a new path – a clear channel that creates separation from what is/was, to what could be. Very SZEN- like if you ask me.

Szenippet: The best way to charge your own engine is to plug into a dream come true before it really does.

■ ■ ■

The Key to Life

Buddy, as his homeless neighbors, cohorts and other transients that lived and begged on the streets knew him, was usually pretty upbeat. When he first arrived he was considered one of the more fortunate of the unfortunates. He was still pretty young by comparison; he had his health and thus was selected from time to time to work on day jobs in construction where he would conveniently be paid in cash for his labor.

Buddy would say that he didn't really have to live on the streets and that he had a plan, but he needed enough money to be able to properly implement it. He liked to report that he always put a little cash away in a safety deposit box at the local bank. The rest went for essentials like food, clothes and diversions – sometimes liquid. Buddy kept the bank key around his neck and would nervously reach for it from time to time to insure he had not lost his ticket to a new life. But those that watched him only saw a rusted skeleton key hanging by a plastic chord. No one ever said a thing to counter his enthusiasm for a new future. Buddy was, after all, the only positive, enthusiastic presence around and he had a way of getting others to start to be positive as well.

Time is never kind to those who live without a home. But Buddy knew he wasn't meant to be where he was and would tell anyone that asked that he was about to move out into his new place and leave the streets behind. The story had not changed in 8 years, but he told it with such conviction that most people on the street half expected that one day, Buddy would simply move away. They always asked him to remember them, his friends that lived next to him all clustered under the overpass.

The days on the street are monotonous with little to do, no funds to go anywhere, with competition for begging, collecting recyclables and the occasional day job. Each of those homeless, living day to day, had their own schedule and no one policed the other. And although Buddy's construction working days had been dwindling over the years he never seemed to be around much during the day. Most assumed he spent his days like everyone else, walking, and hunched over scouring the ground and sidewalks for loose change, discarded lottery tickets or anything else that might be of value.

One night Buddy didn't come back to his cardboard space. There were lots of opinions on why he hadn't returned. Maybe he got arrested, hurt or had just left on his own. After no Buddy for 8 days, a fair waiting period, his "stuff" from his space was split up amongst the remaining street dwellers. As the weeks passed, Buddy's enthusiasm and positive stories, were being missed more and more. A void emerged where there had been a beacon; the smidgeon of hope was now an emptiness felt by all. And within the context of this emptiness, the legend of Buddy and his positive ways grew. It wasn't long before the stories trumped the reality. Speculation and hearsay created unbelievable story lines of how Buddy had managed to escape, leaving behind a whimsical, delicious and totally positive imprint.

The real story is this: The key he wore did fit a lock, but to a door not a box. A door that opened to a room that not only held his childhood memories, but every dream he ever had - A room in an old house where a skeleton key worked just fine. A house that protected Buddy's secrets with a special room that held bank receipts and pay stubs and boxes of memories. A closet with a key next to where his mother sat and waited to hear him and feel his kiss to her cheek. She never knew where he spent his nights, but the money he earned by working and saving by renting his own room to strangers kept her alive. Those extra few years where she couldn't move, but able to talk were filled with stories of love and life and making plans and believing in them. Those were the years that truly changed Buddy's life and well worth his homeless adventure.

Buddy's Mom eventually passed on, but her son and his story is still going strong.

Epilogue
Some years later Buddy passed on too. Shortly thereafter, an official looking gentleman in a business suit visited the homeless turf where Buddy's story was still being passed along to

new members of the less fortunate. The man had a clipboard and a roster of names and he called out each of twenty-two names individually, until a group of 13 huddled around him. Nine, it seems had not outlived Buddy.

The visitor handed each an envelope with an address and cab fare. This would be their new home, compliments of Buddy; it was furnished and ready to live in. They each would be made the legal owner and the only instruction was to help as many others as they felt comfortable doing; it was up to them. Buddy was explicit in his will - his greatest, lasting gift would be the power of choice.

Szenippet: The door to the life you want doesn't need a key.

■ ■ ■

Smoke Brake
From the Szenabling File:

It was one of those cold rainy nights in February - the kind of night where the damp chill seems to penetrate the densest of fabric. The drops of rain felt like they were just moments from turning into ice. He watched the rain drip from the hood of his parka and wondered why in the heck he was standing outside when he could be inside near the fire. As he pulled out his pack of cigarettes and plastic lighter the rain intensified and was beating very hard on the overhang where he stood pinned against the house hoping to avoid as much wetness as possible. Through the noise of the downpour he could hear the crying sound of his five-month-old son inside the house.

This had been his choice, his routine to have a smoke outside regardless of the weather because he wanted to keep the air inside clean for the people he loved. It was a habit and situation that repeated itself way too frequently. He had tried to stop, cut back, switch brands, chew gum, wear a patch, get hypnotized or whatever the latest trend was to arrest his addiction. In the rain, as he lit up once again, he knew that whatever enjoyment smoking may have once provided was gone. The fact that he continued was maddening and getting him pretty wet and cold.

He stuck the last part of the cigarette out into the rain, which snuffed it out. He peered at the butt in his hand and then heard the crying inside turn into a giggle. It made him smile, and he turned back toward the door knowing it was where he needed and where he really wanted to be. And in that knowing, something miraculous happened. When he got inside the house, he picked up his still giggling boy and made himself a promise. That was to be his last cigarette. He never smoked again and strangely never missed it either. He told this story many times and credited his young son's giggle as the catalyst for the "cold turkey" departure from smoking. Whatever it was, it proved that the mind and the body can reach an accord agree to change in an instant.

So what's the secret formula for controlling our desires and bad habits? What do we have to do to unleash the power each of us has to turn the page, a corner, or turn over a new leaf? How do we get rid of the bad stuff and replace it with good? What's blocking our path to greatness and holding us in neutral? Why can't we just change "cold-turkey" into whatever version of us we desire? The answer is within and the key is being honest about the reason why we want to change or why we are terrified to change. Here's why "why" is so important:

Motivation, be it self imposed or coming from an outside source creates a framework for organizing our thoughts. It let's us set priorities. When we're motivated, it's because we see an outcome that is favorable, and we decide that it is worth the energy, time, money, pain etc. to achieve. Essentially, we log whatever that goal is into our internal GPS and move toward it. Once on the move we have to remember and remind ourselves of the "why." Knowing why is empowering and helps us stay focused on the outcome. Focus then helps us create more desire until we reach a tipping point where circumstances, timing and mindset merge to deliver what we seek. Like the rain soaked father being called by his son to change, there will be signs and opportunities directing us to the "you have arrived" point in our lives.

Wherever we are now, we can start to move toward our dream and remember that it's never too late, once we understand "why" we want it.

Szenippet: It just takes a second to change your world.

■ ■ ■

Brand Aid
From the Now & Szen file:

Selling products and services successfully is totally dependent upon how the product or service - the brand - is perceived.

Everything about the brand sends a message and creates an impression. A brand is made up of three distinct components.

1. There is the personality of the people that create or make the brand. Think of the influence a Bill Gates or a Steve Jobs had on their brands.
2. The second component of a brand includes the actual attributes of the product or service. For example a Hilton Hotel is vastly different from a Motel 6, even though they both essentially provide a place to sleep.
3. And the third component of a brand is the image of the user, meaning that the brands we purchase and associate with are a reflection of how we see ourselves. Are you a Motel 6 or Hilton type of person, or somewhere in between? Our choices of the car we drive (import vs. domestic), the stores where we shop (Target vs. Wal-Mart), the clothes we wear (Polo vs. Banana Republic) all say something about us and cumulatively add to our own personal brand.

We are our own brand. Our personality drives the decisions we make, which dictates our individual appearance and value. The subsequent impression created lets others know how they should perceive us. There are so many aspects to the human brand that it's usually difficult to find just one that can really define us. We are more than the sum of our parts. And how we accumulate the pieces takes time and deliberation.

Anywhere along the way we can choose to modify our image if the situation calls for it; like borrowing our parent's car to make an impression on a first date. The new suit, the fitness club we belong to, or the hairstyle and designer labels we select sets the tone and sends messages about how we view ourselves and how we want to be viewed.

And sometimes we need to modify our brand image permanently. Since we're all unique there is no one single way to do this. But if we must, here are a couple of things to consider:

- Start by asking trusted people their impressions of you. You may not even realize what your current brand value is, for good or for bad.
- Begin with a personal vision. Being current with fashion and trends is fine, but usually we evolve into our own personal style, which is often unintentional and based solely on habit. Take a look at what you wear, where you go, whom you hang out with and ask whether it's a true reflection of who you want to be. "New and improved" works with people brands too.
- Not everything we change gets noticed. The new purse or car we get may go unnoticed by our parents, but may send strong signals to co-workers. When modifying our image be mindful of the target.
- Brand loyalty is based on relationships. Everybody that we're close to has an image of us locked in, and they depend on us to maintain the principles that created that image from the beginning. If we are truly serious about modifying our own personal brand, we have to change the perception of others (our brand resides in the minds of others) or we may need to be ready to sever some ties. When or if we get locked into someone else's image of us that we need to change, be aware there is a price.

Because we all share our lives with so many different groups of people, it's possible and very likely that we are perceived differently by each group. And the reason we exist so easily with different settings and people is because on the inside, we're still us. That's why true and lasting change can be difficult. Unlike the brands we buy, the brands we are, last forever; a combination of personality, personal attributes and the image we project. In the end, it's about making an impression; it's our inner voice that tells us who we really are that sets us apart. It's the brand we can trust.

Szenippet: First impressions are sometimes the only ones that last.

■ ■ ■

Help is on the Way

Have you ever had a need to have someone jump-start your car, pick you up at the airport, fix a leaking pipe or just lend you a few dollars in a pinch? In situations like these we sometimes hesitate to make the request. We might think that we should be able to handle it ourselves. Or we might be afraid of the response we'll get. Or that somehow we'll appear weaker for needing the help.

On the other hand when people ask us for assistance we are usually happy to help and are often grateful and flattered that someone felt that they could count on us. I think that we are all actually hard-wired to respond to requests for help and like the feeling we get when we do.

So if you need help with something, don't be afraid to ask. Someone right now would love it if you do.

Szenippet: Saying, "how can I help?" is often stronger than "I love you."

■ ■ ■

Attitude Rules

From the Szenabling file:

I was watching the end of a football game today where one team was ahead most of the game and led with only seconds left. The other team had to score a touchdown to win and had quite a distance to go down the field. Well, just a few plays and seconds later they did just that. They scored on the last play and game over.

This scenario has probably played out millions of times in myriad circumstances and it happens for a very simple reason – attitude. Playing to win is better than playing to not lose. As soon as we play the clock and not the game, we're mentally out of the running. To compete in games and in life, we need to be engaged with a mindset that we will succeed regardless of the time left on the clock.

This is often observed with people that retire and suddenly become ill and pass away. I don't mean to be morbid, but it could be that we all need to have something or someone to drive us. Without motivation, very little can really get accomplished. So whenever we leave something, having something new to get the heart pumping again will help keep us in the game. And it really doesn't matter what is. It's our attitude about it that really matters.

Attitude is our internal view of how we see our role in the universe. When it's positive, we tend to see good outcomes and when it's negative not so much. Attitude is fueled by our belief system, and so if we believe we might lose the game, we start to form a "hang-on" attitude instead of a winning one. Trying to hang-on to anything is like trying to stop the flow, like grasping an ice cube. The more we squeeze and think we have it, the faster it melts. We're left with wet hands and no ice cube.

Here are a few ideas on how to keep our attitude in sync with positive results:

- Stay focused on the goal, not the process, whatever it is.
- Visualize what success would look like **after** you reach the goal. This will also help you set the next one.
- Repeat as needed.

Szenippet: Having time without purpose can be the catalyst and opportunity for positive change or the beginning of a slide into permanent neutral.

■ ■ ■

En Garde
A Sixty-Word SZEN Story:

There was no way that Marcus would make the appointment on time. He started early, but ran into traffic, and then almost there, he realized he forgot the prototype. He became a bit reckless as he darted around cars, now on his second effort to get to the meeting of his life. Miraculously he made it. Shaken, but very ready.

And more...
Some people are so focused that nothing can dissuade them from their goal. Obstacles, setbacks, restarts, etc. - it doesn't matter what they encounter they overcome and succeed. They feed on the stress for success, and it just seems to make them stronger. Is it the training, knowledge, education, experience, or just plain luck that makes the difference? Maybe a little bit of each, but mostly what separates the "always ready" from the "still chasing" is not so much about the *what* as it is about the *when*.

We've all heard the expression "timing is everything" which implies that somehow good fortune puts us in just the right place and time to take advantage of an opportunity. And of course that does happen, but for the ever successful, never thwarted, and bound and determined success-chaser, it's not really about a timely event or coincidence that generates luck, it's about all of the lucky and incredible moments that lead to it.

Here's the rule: No moment should ever be taken for granted. This sounds pretty simple and probably not a bad idea, but for most of us we pack a zillion moments into each and every day that we let pass by without notice. It's easy to rationalize that not every experience in the "now" will net something positive and incredible, so we pick and choose when to be alert and En Garde. That's a big difference from Marcus who remained so present and aware that even under stress he attached himself to the very second where he stood and in that moment there is a calmness, grounding and internal readiness. The real beauty of this perspective is that all of us, by simply paying just a little bit more attention to the now and less to the then or when, can capture real life, drama, happiness and good fortune right when we need it most, which of course is always.

Szenippet: All moments have an equal chance at changing our lives.

■ ■ ■

No Will No Way
A Sixty-Word SZEN Story:

The leaves crackled under his step breaking the dark silence. He reached for the door and opened it slowly. Peering down the dimly lit hallway he looked and listened intently for a sign, sound, or a sense, and stepped inside. He felt the whoosh of the door slamming and froze. Fear swept in, but his will prevailed, leading the way.

And more...
Being bold in the face of fear doesn't diminish the fear, but rather puts it in its place. Taking the steps we want, making the moves we seek, pushing our needle of success forward are all examples of following the will of our inner self, regardless of any fear or the obstacles seen or unseen. The willpower we posses is an incredible yet very complex system for making things happen – good things, bad things, any things.

Things occur because when we seek outcomes and put energy toward them. We literally create and draw people and circumstances to our aid. Often the grander the goal the more willpower it takes, but sometimes, good luck helps us too. The opposite of willpower is "won't power." We use this when we are wishing "against" an outcome – something bad or we somehow fear that is about to happen, might happen or maybe something that will never happen ever; it's all in how we see it. Won't power happens by simply turning off the *will* to let something just happen on its own. This lack of positive willpower looks a lot like indifference, where no effort nets nothing, no gain, or even loss.

Both options are always available and they play significant roles in our life. Generally speaking though, anything we put our energy toward will thrive and grow and what we ignore will wither and die. And all throughout the process, we control the flow of "will" which is why there are no accidents in life. So doing "nothing" will also impact how life unfolds. Yes, it's complicated, but it's also a huge gift to be able to point to and then keep moving toward our dream whether the path is scary or not and even if the door slams behind us.

Szenippet: Willpower is desire in motion.

■ ■ ■

Rain of Fear
From the Now & Szen file:

A while ago I visited the Museum of Modern Art in New York. They have a special exhibit called the Rain Room. In this room, it rains everywhere except where you are standing, even if you move it follows and stops. Rain all around, but not on you. It's the antithesis of the dark cloud following one around and a totally satisfying metaphor for those die-hard optimists that, even when completely drenched, never lose their positive view of their world.

I like to think I'm one of those *glass mostly full* types. So every day I fill up the glass and enter the world of unknown events and circumstances. A place that an encounter with other like - minded people is a possibility and always a joy when it happens. Sometimes, the glass just runs over.

Then of course there are the *mostly empty glass* types. When I encounter these types, I try to share what's in my glass. I sometimes pour it on, so to speak, to help resist the negative pull. Unfortunately it often doesn't help and I sense that their glass has a large hole in it somewhere. They can't hold what they don't seek, and they become so contrary that would likely get very wet, even in the Rain Room.

I think one reason that people hold on to the half empty perspective is fear - Fear to trust, fear to believe and fear of the unknown. It's easier to retreat when you're afraid. But it's exactly the time when courage is required. And even though it is raining all around us, we can sometimes, and more often than we think, take a step into the downpour and never feel a drop.

Szenippet: Always begin your song on a positive note.

■　■　■

CHAPTER ONE EDITOR'S NOTES – A PREVIEW

AT WORK

Anchors Away (if you get stagnant in life and work, you may miss opportunities)

Incentive Claws (decide what your path is…risk taking or risk adverse)

Holiday Math (not sure if I would include this one at all. Its one of the few that's kind of negative)

Why Not (overcoming cul de sac thinking)

It May not be What you Think

Neatness Counts (presentation is an important part of everything)

Think Fast (staying present will help you think on your feet)

Risk Management (I liked this one. It's almost the same advice, though you give in On the Fence.)

Let's Meet Again (Things may not always go the way we plan, be prepared for the next opportunity)

Anchor Away

From the Szenabling File:

Josh had been a good reporter with an eye for news, tempered with real empathy for those who found themselves reluctantly in the headlines. He was the kind of person that people felt they could talk to. As a reporter this served him well, and so when the executive producer told him that he was in line to become the evening news anchor, he was pleased, but not surprised.

Josh had learned the news by working a beat for the daily newspaper. When one is reporting for a newspaper they know that the broadcasters in their market would jump on whatever it was that they could uncover and get printed into the morning edition. Josh would often smile as he heard the radio news reporting on something that he had discovered and reported on, but they had taken to be their exclusive. The fact was that most of the radio and TV stations routinely got their news from the morning paper. When Josh was hired away to work on one of the local TV independent's news programs, he felt strangely distanced from the real news; less a reporter, and more of a "talent." But again, his empathy proved to be a valuable asset and when people would tell him stories *on camera* they did so with a real desire to let what they were feeling be exposed.

For the last few years, Josh had worked his empathetic magic into numerous awards including some local Emmys. Although still quite young by comparison to other seasoned news professionals, Josh had become the heir apparent for Richard who had commanded the evening news anchor chair for over 18 years. This year, Richard had suffered from some medical problems, which produced a chronic and raspy cough that clipped his words and slowed his presentation; his usual crisp delivery of the day's important stories and issues had lost its intensity. Everybody at the station and in the industry knew that it was only a matter of time before he'd step down. For Josh, it couldn't come soon enough.

Josh patiently waited and did his normal in-depth coverage of the day's stories of the people that created and were affected by the goings on of the world. Meanwhile, Richard, raspy cough and all, had grown big in the ratings, which seemed to give him a new source of energy and pride. Richard would boast that as the oldest anchor in the market he still brought in the biggest audience. The executive producer would shrug his shoulders when Josh would inquire about the timing for taking the reins. Two years had passed since that first hint that he would take command. Over that time he had resisted other offers and opportunities and had unwittingly sunk into a holding pattern fueled by what he discerned to be high, and real expectations for his future.

Richard amazingly continued for another 6 years and when Josh's time finally came he was passed over by someone younger and untainted by being the guy waiting in the wings. Josh was told that he had lost his edge and seemed to be too passive for the position. What Josh had expected and wanted to happen never did. And in that waiting he had lost opportunities and inexplicably his drive. Waiting for, and expecting something to happen can freeze a person into a stall. It's why expectations need to be tempered by frequent reality checks.

Is there something you're waiting for? Something promised, negotiated, obvious and unavoidable? Think again.

Nothing is for sure until it's already happened. Setting expectations is normal and necessary, but relying on them to take fruition can be dangerous and risky. The new job, promotion, new contract, raises or whatever we think is inevitable may simply never happen.

The reason expectations often don't materialize is that they require actions from other people, and as we all know, no one can ever predict the actions of another. When we hold on to a desired outcome too long, we can become stuck and in a waiting posture and we become less creative. The best we can do is to stay focused on our goals yet remain open to possibilities. Remember that even though we can't control the actions of others, their actions might be exactly what we need and that's an outcome we can live with but never predict.

Szenippet: The bank of the unknown must clear an expectation before it's added to your account.

■ ■ ■

Incentive Claws
From the Szenabling File:

The job sounded pretty good to Tony. The salary wasn't as much as he was used to, but the opportunity for a huge performance bonus and ownership in the company made it quite appealing. He struggled with the decision and vacillated between staying where he was with the security of knowing what he would earn versus the possibility of really breaking the bank and having a *piece of the pie*. He took the position.

He began to share with family and friends what he had decided. He learned quickly that there are different schools of thought when it comes to taking a risk. Some people believe that the security of a consistent and predictable income is the only way to go. They will tell you how much easier it is to sleep at night knowing that their job, income and life are in order. They can see their retirement fund, savings and net worth growing and relish the freedom that this prudent approach provides. They budget and enjoy the fruits of their labor with regular vacations, high credit scores and reduced stress. And when they are older and have the time to really get away they will do it without any financial worries. Tony completely understood their thinking, as it was exactly his life up until he took the new job. He had entered another school of thought – the "opportunity of a lifetime" school.

After a few short months at work, Tony began to understand that what his new position lacked in security, it made up for in excitement. The problem he was having was that "excitement" wasn't paying the rent. And after work, away from the high energy, hi tech, newest, greatest widget environment that ran on adrenaline, he found himself at home, alone with a pile of bills and a microwave dinner. Not surprisingly though, Tony really liked the new gig and looked forward to going to work every day. His work was no longer was a job, but more like a mission. He found his spot and decided he would see it through; he visualized the bonus, the stock and the glory – just a happy, albeit temporarily poorer version of himself.

What happened to Tony happens to many people. They may be okay with what's happening in their lives, but sense there might be more out there than they realize. Some choose to stay where they are: happy with their life and future. Others leave and try another path. Both ways can work, and depending on the kind of person we find ourselves to be, or even dream to be, both offer real potential for happiness. One choice is not better than another, only different. The difference is found in what makes each of us get up and go every day. What motivates us is the combination of joy, earnings, opportunity, freedom, praise, wealth, responsibility etc.

The fact is, we're all incentivized by something. We all have an inner voice that drives us, and once we hear its calling, we engage on the path that feels most right to us. The key word here is "most." Anyone can be tempted to wander from his or her chosen path, but something inside us brings us back. Like Tony, we have a choice and as with so many things in life, we can't know the results until the end; which of course may come sooner than we think. So choose well and remember to enjoy your choices not just for the end result, but for the journey along the way.

Szenippet: If what makes you go, makes you sad, don't go.

■ ■ ■

Holiday Math

Leave it to the ingenuity of Americans to take a single holiday day off and turn it into an extended mental leave of absence; it's called holiday math. Everybody, it seems, is involved in stretching a single Monday into two weeks of downtime. This is truly an art because it is all done in a type of collective hypnosis. It is a simple planting of a seed and a notion that because our world (United States) will be closed on Monday we must prepare for it mentally in advance and then recover from it in the same way. By turning one day into two weeks we demonstrate the power of focused and positive thinking.

We accomplish this by looking ahead to the upcoming day off – such as Labor Day - which always falls on a Monday. We see it coming as early as the Monday before and begin to strategize how we can get an "early start" by leaving early from work on Friday or maybe beginning the "l-o-n-g" weekend on Thursday night. This pretty much eliminates Thursday as any kind of productive day at all. That makes Wednesday into the last day of the week and thus creates a wonderful week-end euphoria that mentally begins on the Monday before the break. In fact the entire week, our minds become ever more vacation conscious making it extremely difficult to cram what has become already a short week into two and ½ days.

Of course a measly two and ½ days is not enough time to do the really big projects. So all of the departments start to cut back on the schedules knowing that it's futile to accomplish so much in so little time. Some people will also add a vacation day, thus maximizing the total time that they take off. As people begin to talk about plans for the holiday, this enormous power of suggestion takes hold of everyone in the organization, which is now on holiday watch, all sharing a psychologically shortened countdown to "quitting time." This mental euphoria of course, spills out into other organizations until the contamination is complete. And of course if you are lucky enough to take a sick day anytime during the week, it is like getting an entire week's vacation. The net result is that by Thursday afternoon business pretty much slows for everyone and is nearly non-existent by Friday. We forget that there will be a price to pay on the flip side.

The actual holiday itself seems like a Sunday all day and so we conveniently forget that the upcoming week will be a "short" week. Tuesday finally comes after the virtual "week off" and so it seems like an extra hung-over version of a normal Monday. There is added pressure however, because by not having a normal Monday to recuperate, it means we're already in the hole for the week. This backs up the work until Wednesday which can't be finished on time, making Thursday filled with impossible deadlines that threaten to get in the way of our normal light Friday. When Friday arrives, we're exhausted from the two weeks off and vow to get some rest over the weekend to prepare for the following week, which looms as being extra busy because everyone has been putting off whatever they could.

All that said, this week's Book of Szen has now slipped into a Monday instead of its pseudo normal Saturday or Sunday. But it really seems like a Sunday, so I'm not really late at all and probably way ahead of many of you that missed last week's edition because you were thinking about today's day off last week and missed it. Either way I don't know what I was thinking or why I'm writing on a holiday anyway. Given the upcoming short week, no one will have time to read it anyway. I could have been using holiday math to plan for a vacation or simply stress out about tomorrow, which is coming way too fast, don't you think?

Szenippet: Thinking about doing something is the first step to getting it done; and usually the most important.

■ ■ ■

Why Not?
How to overcome cul-de-sac thinking
From the Buszeniness file:

One of the rules for a good old-fashioned brainstorming session is that there are no bad ideas. All ideas are equal and deserve discussion and analysis. To quickly eliminate concepts is not the goal of the meeting, but rather to think beyond the status quo and consider a *why not* perspective. Often the current situation is like a cul-de-sac, in which there is no way to go except the way you came. This creates a *why we can't* mentality.

In the *why we can't* school of thinking, many good ideas are discounted because it's not obvious *how* they could get done. This roadblock reasoning assumes the path that needs to be taken is filled with roadblocks and obstacles beyond our current capability. In other words, we're stuck in our tracks. In the *why we can't* world, every brainstorming session begins with a discussion of what's wrong, and spirals down from there. The truism that emerges is that once something begins on a negative note, it's difficult to shift. What's strange, and a bit sad, is that some of these meetings are actually deemed successful because the existing direction was confirmed: "Great meeting team, we've established that we are definitely on the path to failure."

In the *why not* world, ideas are explored and new ones added, and variations on a theme are stretched and explored with a view toward a positive outcome. When we keep focused on the goals rather than the process, we're able to uncover greater opportunities. The corresponding positive attitude that emerges can actually be the catalyst to make an idea really come to life. That's because once we believe it's possible, we actually draw the strength, support, and good fortune we need to achieve. Many entrepreneurs, inventors, and innovators attained success with their dreams without having a clue on how they would get there: "I don't know how just yet, but I've got to try."

Here are a couple of thoughts to help us uncover or create the next great *whatever:*

- No ideas exist in isolation. Whatever the possibilities might be, remember that we may not be the only ones thinking this way. Often a good idea appears from multiple sources, simultaneously, and in unexpected places. Its refinement is often collaborative.
- Hold that thought. As we think about our own *why not* idea we often bump into a solution that was waiting there all along. By simply thinking about the goal, we attract the means to make it happen.
- Keep the door open. To accept good fortune and luck we have to stay alert and flexible; we may even have to turn around. We never know how a simple suggestion or a twist on a phrase can change our world.

Whatever the journey, we can only get *there* from here, once we are able to see *there.*

Szenippets: The road to success is sometimes filled with *You* - turns.

If fear knocks at your door and you don't answer, it will temporarily retreat, but if you face it, it will never come back.

■ ■ ■

It May Not Be What You Think

Ben, also known as "Benny the Bean Counter" checked his email for the message. He was hitting the *fetch mail* button every few seconds and scanning the *from* column for the name he so desperately wanted to see. Where was it he wondered, why was there no response?

He slumped down in his chair feeling detached, alone and anxious. For Ben, waiting was never something he did very well. That's part of why he became such a gifted and sought after CFO. He would rarely ponder any decisions when it came to numbers. He was fast acting and notoriously accurate when it came to matters of finance and economics. "Numbers never lie" he would say, "but they have a shelf life and they can turn impatient quickly or worse, become atrophied if not acted upon." Ben believed that numbers had a power because they obeyed the rules and that *everything* was quantifiable. In Ben's world he trained himself to suppress his true nature of always trusting his instincts and instead preached that everything had to add up and nothing was random. Looking back at his *inbox* he began to consider that he had made a miscalculation. He reached into his desk, rummaging for the bottle of aspirin.

Thousands of miles away, the proposal that Ben had anguished over – a chance to take a much respected tech company public, lay on Richard's desk. Every line and every calculation had been scrutinized. In a word, the recommendation was *flawless* and this was exactly what bothered Richard and why he hesitated to hit the *reply* button. Of the numerous candidates for CFO Richard considered, Ben was by far the most qualified, but something had troubled Richard during the interview: Ben seemed too much the perfectionist and didn't seem to be engaging or friendly enough. It wasn't that Richard was looking for a new best friend, but he knew that whomever he brought on board he'd not only have to trust, but he would need to like him too and so would the rest of the team. That's why the reply was delayed and Richard waited for the last one on the list of Ben's previous employers to call him – it was Ben's first boss out of college.

Catherine had hired Ben and made him and assistant in the accounting department. He worked for her for over 8 years and she hesitated to tell Richard the story of how Ben's mistake had cost her company dearly. As references go, it was a real negative. As Catherine told it, Ben was well liked, friendly, outgoing and open-minded, but lacked discipline and took more time than other people in the department to do the job. She categorized young Ben as a dreamer and not really cut out to be working with numbers. She was sorry, but could not recommend him. It was exactly what Richard wanted to hear and he immediately picked up the phone and called Ben.

Ben read the email from Catherine telling him that she was sorry that she could not endorse him for the position he sought. Simultaneously the phone rang and surprised to hear Richard on the line, Ben began to unravel. This was not going at all the way he thought it would go and he began to utter soft apologies, but not sure why. Catherine's email had undone his aspirations, and he struggled to find the calmness and words to talk to Richard. After rambling for a minute or so Ben paused and then listened in shock as Richard welcomed him to the team. Same Ben, two perspectives: Catherine did not know the Ben he had become and Richard needed to know the Ben he once was.

Sometimes the most disparate actions, events and commentary can join to create an unexpected yet clear picture of what was meant to be. We can find common cause and the unpredictable crossing of paths where we never thought they could or should be. People from our past often serve to launch us into a new and exciting future. Everything we've done or are about to do comes together eventually and like Ben, pieces of our story from long ago can come forward once more- reminding us that what we think is not always the same as who we are.

Szenippet: In the world of the unknown, all possibilities exist.

■ ■ ■

Neatness Counts

When I was attending college I was also working a lot of hours, and from time to time I would miss a class and have to rely on my friends to take good notes. It was a reciprocal arrangement that worked out fine most of the time. It is interesting that by using someone else's notes we are limited to only the information that they feel is important. It's a bit like reading a review of a movie when you have no clue to its plot. And when the notes were the only source of input and both people had to write an essay on the subject matter, it became a challenge to not only write it well, but to be different from what the other person would present.

Enter the typewriter. By typing the essay and then packaging it in a colorful folder, I found that my essay stood out from the standard hand-written submissions by most other students. Sometimes I would receive an "A" based on my friend's notes and he, who actually attended the class, would get a "B." This experience was really a life lesson for me. Understanding how we all are influenced by how things are "packaged" (you could substitute the word *branded*) has turned out to be my life's work.

I share this because this weekend I'm grading final projects for my branding class and I have to say that that whole colorful folder thing still works.

Szenippet: Appearances can be deceiving only because we are so accepting of what we initially perceive. Sadly, we often don't have the time to dig further.

■ ■ ■

Think Fast
A Sixty-Word SZEN Story:

Bill was nervous about his final interview. He'd been told that this CEO was no nonsense. Sitting at the conference room table, he saw the many awards and accolades this company had achieved. Landing a job here would change everything. Suddenly the CEO entered, holding his phone and took a "selfie" of him and Bill. Bill laughed. The CEO didn't.

And more...
Things that happen to us when we're not ready for them test us in ways that expose our true nature and self-concept. When there is no time to make a considered and thoughtful decision, we're left with only two options to rely on: instinct or training.

Training is the bailiwick of coaches, emergency responders, the military and almost anything or anyone we can think of where it is beneficial, if not critical to be *ready*. This includes situations found in politics or even a job interview like Bill's, who probably prepared very well for his CEO meeting based on the "norms" for such a thing. Pre-planning and preparedness are helpful and at the core of the curriculum of most training program. They should be very much a part of our own individual approach to taking on something new, strange, or very important. Most of us don't like to be surprised.

When we are surprised, however, we often have no time to think and so whatever reaction we have is all we have. Reacting to random, unpredictable circumstances or events draws our personal history and understanding of our own nature front and center. We may have only a split second to assimilate and act, and what we decide is often final.

So what can we do to be really ready for whatever? To be better prepared for the unknown requires a clear commitment to the now. When we are present, we are all there and that's an advantage in just about everything we do. The more we are "aware" the more we absorb what's around us and the better our senses engage and respond and that gives us an edge - Enough of an edge sometimes to meet surprise with wisdom; Wisdom born from a calmness that only we can create.

Szenippet: What we need to do when we can't see something coming at us is often visible in our hearts long before we need to react.

■ ■ ■

Risk Management
A Sixty-Word SZEN Story:

Brian won all of the awards, was a huge success and admired by his peers, teammates, clients and even the competition. He had advanced to the head of global sales. However with an interim CEO taking over for Brian's friend and mentor, who had passed suddenly, Brian could feel the tension. The culture and future was shifting - not "feeling" right.

And more...
We all know examples where someone enters a situation or even just walks into the room and the entire feeling changes. Sometimes the mood will lighten and sometimes it will become heavy. Some people just seem to have the power to shift the energy of those they come into contact with. Often this is the leader or boss whose confidence or position

commands attention, but it can be anyone whose energy and focus is high.

In nearly every human encounter there is the possibility of a power play to emerge where personalities collide and fight for dominance. Like Brian, who begins to feel a shift, we can tell when something is changing or amiss. And if we are not in a position to control the situation, we become at risk. And once we identify what we're feeling we can then decide how to respond. The response will set the tone for all future encounters. Here are some options:

- Don't respond. Try to be neutral and ignore what you're sensing and hope that it will pass. Eventually we can conform to whatever is impacting our space.
- Retreat. Unlike not responding, a retreat leads us to avoid situations where we experience a feeling or condition we don't like. A retreat is a negative response and puts us on guard, which can cause stress.
- Take control. Choose to modify our behavior so that we can feel in charge of our emotions. This is especially helpful in a work situation where a new boss or policy is making us uneasy. We may know we can't change the problem at the source but we can decide on how we view it. Taking control of our feelings will help to keep us grounded.

I like the last option the most because it lets us set our own course. We may choose to exit, conform or fight to avoid the risk of having to endure a negative situation, but we will retain the power, which is always a better option. With power we can change course and lives too, especially our own.

Szenippet: We can anticipate a risk and maneuver around it, but if we stop too long to dwell on it, it stymies our growth and may catch us in our tracks.

■ ■ ■

Let's Meet Again
A Sixty-Word SZEN Story:

Danny was last on the agenda. HR ran long on their presentation on proper "management speak" and the sales manager was now stuck on a question from the CEO on "sandbagging." With a "hard stop" in a few minutes, Danny knew his inaugural presentation would be cut short. When his time finally came there was no time; maybe next time.

And more...
What happened to Danny can happen to anyone. We get ready to share or present or tell someone something. But suddenly we're abruptly silenced and the moment is passed. We may have practiced and fretted in preparation, and we may have crafted and rehearsed the exact perfect string of words and concepts for our audience. But when it doesn't happen, the energy and the timing is lost. The next opportunity is never quite the same as the first and that's because we're not the same.

When we're ready and prepared to accomplish something significant, our whole nervous system and mental balance becomes aligned and focused on the goal. And if for some reason, the meeting or the game or the date etc. doesn't happen, we lose an advantage that positive energy can bring. That's because the process of anticipation creates adrenalin, which helps us get excited. And if the plug is pulled, that excitement and enthusiasm has no place to go, or does it?

There is a good chance we can recall the excitement and be ready for the next opportunity. Here are some thoughts:

- Reframe the change in plans by recognizing that whatever you wanted to accomplish is still possible. Try not to judge the change in timing as a negative sign. It's just a change.
- With the possibility still ahead of us, we can start to build momentum in advance with the advantage of being more prepared. And because we know what we know even better, the outcome could be better too.
- Remember that timing is everything and so embrace the next scheduled encounter as proof that the timing will be right when it's right, whenever it happens.

Another chance is all Danny and all we ever need to succeed, whenever it comes.

Szenippet: If you doubt your power to change the way you are, you dismiss the creator inside that can show you what you really can do when you set your mind to it.

■ ■ ■

Hidden but Sought
From the Szenabling file:

A couple had been driving for quite some time on a long and somewhat boring trip through the desert. After a few hours the woman asked the man if he wanted to stop and take a break. He said, no, I'm good to go another couple of hours.

She folded her arms and looked straight ahead and it only took a few moments for the driver to notice the cold silence.

He pulled into the next rest stop, feeling the vibe that she wanted a break all along.

Some questions and comments are worth a second reading. Often, people mask other agendas or needs and prefer to take the indirect route, hoping we can translate their comments into the real issue. So questions like "are you thirsty yet?" means I'm thirsty now. We can substitute almost any word for thirsty. Or "I'm really going to try" could mean they are going to try, or they don't think they can succeed or possibly they are saying they need help. Taking another person's comments or request as the obvious and literal version can sometimes mean we miss the real point.

This is easier to spot in person versus text or email because there are always unspoken non-verbal signs that reveal the real. And then of course there are people that are absolutely literal and when they say they don't want us to help clean the kitchen, they mean it, although I think that might be rare. In any case, here are 3 things we can do to be sure:

- Listen and read between the lines. Are you hearing what they said or what you want to hear?
- Confirm and rephrase. Do you mean this or this?

- Respond and ask a confirming question. "I don't need a break, we're making good time, but we can stop if you'd like. Would you like to stop?"

If the person says no, stop anyway. See above.

Szenippet: "I know what you mean" shifts the focus to you while "I understand" keeps the discussion on point. Choose carefully. ----

■ ■ ■

CHAPTER ONE EDITOR'S NOTES – A PREVIEW

WITH OTHERS

Hidden But Sought (ask why to get the answers behind the answers)

Holiday Gathering (appreciate those who are in your life at the holidays)

Casting Call (choose the characters in your movie well)

Coming Around Again (let go of your old traumas to find new love)

Assumptive Algorithm (don't make assumptions when you are trying to understand. Replay messages)

What If (ask for what you want clearly and you are more likely to receive it.)

Express Lane (expressions and connections are the most important things)

A Knew Day (paying attention in the present helps us focus, but can become boring if we don't have something to challenge us and keep us guessing)

Some Buddy Will (relying on Friends)

Silent Sequel (similar to other stories about staying on the path or taking an new course.)

Holiday Gathering

Wherever we may find ourselves, and with whomever we are sharing the holiday with, remember that the lives of those hands we hold around the table have arrived for a reason. Our path and the paths of those we celebrate with have led to this moment. It's a time to reflect on the good fortune and luck to be together and safe, and to be grateful for what we have and hopeful in the journey ahead.

Szenippet: Where we are is not the same as who we are. Only our heart knows the difference.

■ ■ ■

Casting Call

When we study a script and get to know the characters, we often are able to visualize a specific person that would be perfect for a particular part. A certain genre of movie for example, be it action hero, romantic interlude, or even crass comedy conjures up a selected few names that we all would recognize and appreciate. So often movies are built around a specific actor based on previous work, that the actor becomes type cast. And yet there are some well-known actors that freely and easily move in an out of disparate roles and always deliver a totally believable performance.

If we are to consider that in our own personal script, we need to have certain characters to bring it to life and to help us on our journey. We may not start by casting a specific person, but probably a very specific type of person. We might choose the types of people we need based on our own experience and any individual role models we may have. Another important aspect of creating our own plot is to understand the opening scene and the first few chapters. So much of our story is written before we have control over the dialogue and direction.

At some point, we get to choose to continue with the story we started with, or somehow alter the plot and create a new story and rethink the characters, location and the narrative. Even without any rewrites, our lives tend to continue on a set course and shift at certain intervals like leaving home, graduating, getting married, having children etc. Thus our roles shift as well from being student to spouse to parent etc. And in those roles we might even become typecast ourselves, which is neither good nor bad, it just is.

Occasionally, as our metaphorical movie unfolds, we face change. Maybe a cast member is suddenly lost, a new one added or perhaps there is one cast member in our life that just can't seem to fit the role we had in mind for them. When something or someone doesn't seem to fit our story we struggle and like good directors we try to get the best performance we can from what we have to work with. Sometimes we get lucky and make it through, sometimes not. If not, we may have to search for someone new to fill a key role or possibly rethink the ending to the story. When looking for someone to join in, to help create, our own life's Oscar party, keep a few things in mind:

- Happy endings attract. Just because certain things haven't worked out to this point doesn't mean they won't; try to stay positive.
- Consider recycling. Maybe a character present in earlier chapters foreshadowed a clue as to how the story will end and they could be seamlessly reintroduced.
- Advertise. Let people know what we're looking for. Include experience, temperament, and ability to take direction.
- Be open-minded. A new member of our own life's cast of characters can have a dramatic and profound impact on the story. But so can any member of the existing cast, if we're open to it. The best directors listen to their actors.

Now that I've milked this movie analogy to death, I'll end with a quote from Samuel Goldwyn: "No person who is enthusiastic about his work has anything to fear from life."

Szenippet: Having a fulfilling relationship can happen for us anytime, with anyone, as long as we don't insist on who it is.

■ ■ ■

Coming Around Again

"I want to be able to hear a love song and see a face," she said to no one in earshot, as the music seemed to overtake the room and the mood.

Melanie had spent the last few hours scouring the photos and profiles of so many men on-line that it seemed like a blur, and the music was making it even cloudier. What she really wanted wasn't clear to her just yet, but she for sure knew what she didn't want. Facial hair, turned around baseball caps and bare chests were all signs to hit delete. Also anybody that was promising to be moving to her hometown of Seattle in just a few weeks did not make the short list either. The problem was that the short list was really short.

Melanie had met a few guys over coffee in a "meet and greet" format. Usually within a nanosecond she knew if there would be date two. So far, after a couple of months, nobody made it to the second round.

There were, however, a few encounters though that initially seemed promising, but ended abruptly, the same way: The conversation would be fluid and she would freely be sharing details of her broken romance with Robert, always making the point that she didn't understand exactly why it had to end. After all, she had told her lost love many times over the years just how great it was for her, and what it meant to her to have him in her life. It was always at this stage of the conversation where she found herself smiling and thinking to herself: "this could be good." And then, just at that moment, she would see the disconnect in her date's eyes. He had checked out, and without much more than polite conversation, the date was over.

She wondered what was causing these seemingly perfect matches to get up and leave right at the moment she was feeling most connected. She played back the dialogue in her mind, searching for clues and eventually came to understand that it wasn't only what she was saying, it was what she was not saying that was oozing out and changing the mood of the meeting. As she replayed her words over and over and over she began to see and feel for herself what these *first dates* could sense immediately; it was the feeling of anger and resentment. But why?

The real epiphany for Melanie came as she discovered the unnerving reality of her relationship with Robert was that she was the only one actually *in* the relationship. She was always the one that would articulate the love they felt for each other and how strong and special it was. She was always starting conversations with "I love you." And now a few painful months had passed and she knew that she alone had been doing the work to make it go and grow. She alone saw a future in the relationship. Now in the process of reliving those four years, she honestly could recall only a few words, or gestures or signs that ever confirmed that Robert was on board and just as committed. Wow, talk about a reality check.

Once Melanie understood all this, she could let go, and finally hit the restart button. As the music once again floated to the surface – "...and I believe in love, and who knows where or when, but it's coming around again..." - she began to see the face in the love song; it was she.

Szenippet: Sometimes we come out of love empty handed, which makes it easier to grasp the next time.

Szenippet: People can't help you when they don't know you need it.

■ ■ ■

Assumptive Algorithm

There is a wonderful book by Miguel Ruiz entitled *The Four Agreements* - Four things we can do to lead a better, more enriched life. One of the four agreements is "Don't Make Assumptions." Here is what the author says: "Find the courage to ask questions and to express what you really want. Communicate with others as clearly as you can to avoid misunderstandings, sadness and drama. With just this one agreement, you can completely transform your life." I totally agree that it is desirable to not assume anything, because an assumption quickly becomes a belief and it's our beliefs, accurate or not, that determine how we see ourselves and the world we live in. That said, the world is spinning so fast that we've become accustomed to assuming. Making assumptions, jumping to conclusions and believing we're right saves us time and stress, or so we think. Here's how it works:

A (Message Sent)　　　　=　**B** (Message Received)
B (Message Received) =　**C** (Message Understood)
∴ **(Therefore)**
A (Message Sent)　　　　=　**C** (Message Understood)

A while ago, I sent a signed copy of my Book of Szen to a friend in Florida. A few months went by and I received an email that said that she never received the book. I had sent it **(A)** and actually had been wondering why I had not heard back or anything like maybe "thanks, I love it." She was thinking I was maybe too busy to send it, or changed my mind or just forgot. I had assumed she got it. She had assumed I had not sent it **(A** never happened). And therefore we both believed something that was not a complete truth (**B** and **C** were missing). I sent another, which she received and then the first book showed up in the mail a few days later. I'm not making this stuff up.

What about the experience of sending or texting a message and not getting a response? We could easily (or maybe we have from time to time) jump to a conclusion that the other person is being rude because they obviously don't care and are just ignoring us. What can happen sometimes is technology fails us and the message never got there. A friend just told me that she recently rebooted her smart phone and miraculously messages she had never seen appeared – some were very important and even critical too. It's the same equation as above – **B** never happens so there can't be a **C**.

The two examples I just gave can be easily explained and perhaps no harm is done. But what of the situation where the person sending the message believes that their intention is understood? This means that if two people or two companies (I've seen this before) or maybe two countries believe they understand each other, but they really don't, it could be a recipe for disaster.

The implications of making assumptions in relationship are profound. Anywhere along the way, if one misunderstands the other and then acts upon it, it can create layers of misperception and wrong thinking. Here's what the author says: "Just imagine the day you stop making assumptions with your partner and eventually with everyone else in your life. Your way of communicating will change completely, and your relationships will no longer suffer from conflicts by mistaken assumptions."

What's needed is another step– Message Confirmed. The reason this is important is because in step **B** where the message is received is also where a person lives. People have biases, preconceived notions, are too busy, don't understand or misread the message altogether. There are endless possibilities when people get involved. It's also possible that the timing of the message finds the receiver in an off mood and so he/she sends a return message that seems to be completely out of context. The bottom line is that there are countless opportunities to miscommunicate and much of it starts with the belief that we have everything we need to know to make a judgment. There has to be a better way.

Here's a different model. It's not just the movement of information; it's the understanding that ultimately defines us.

A (Message Sent)
B (Message Received)
C (Message Replayed/Understood)
= **D** (Message Confirmed)

∴ **(Therefore)**
Happy Endings (I assume you know what I mean)

It might be more work, but could also be just the thing to change our lives...

Express Lane
A Sixty-Word SZEN Story:

It was standing room only and the conversations were all stretched to cut through the din. Pete could only see about 3 people deep and although he scoured the room, he could not locate the face of his future. He knew she was there and this time he had to try. Suddenly she appeared: Eye contact - no blinking allowed.

And more...
Communication can take many forms with most of it being non-verbal. Body language, facial expressions, finger tapping and eye-to-eye contact can tell the most intimate of stories and either add credence to or negate whatever words we might choose to use. Our body will always give us away and reveal the real message we want to send. That's why a genuine smile can melt hearts and will almost always generate a return smile, while folded arms indicate that this person is closed to communication.

Expressions, in addition to words, are so needed to connect that we've developed an entire sub-language of symbols, smiles and winks to support the condensed and often fractured text we tend to rely on to make our points via texting, emails, and social media. Yet, for all of our advancements in technology, nothing serves us better in getting through than a direct express lane to another - where eyes can meet and link. They've been called the windows to the soul and so they are. Looking directly at someone tells him or her you're focused and you mean what you're projecting.

When Pete found her, all he needed was to connect his gaze to hers, and in the briefest of interludes, feelings, desires, questions and hope flowed freely. And without a word, the face of his future smiled and so did he – All in favor...! Yes, the "eyes" have it.

Szenippet: Seeing the world through wide-open eyes can not only bring what's coming next into focus, but often change our view of the past.

■ ■ ■

Some Buddy Will

A Sixty-Word SZEN Story:

The group was going full steam up the mountain, impervious to the dangerous outgrowth, loose gravel and sinkholes that would have slowed any normal expedition. Not these women. They prided themselves on hiking to the highest peaks and across the most barren, treacherous landscapes on the planet. Tracy however kept falling behind and eventually out of sight. Would they return?

And more...
Having faith in our team, relationship, partners or friends allows all of us to venture into new territory with a sense of confidence. Knowing someone has got our back means a lot especially when treading into new, unknown, territory. The concept of the "buddy system" – watching out for and taking care of our teammate or partner and knowing they will do the same, can open the door to journeys that many of us would never take alone. Just the idea that someone is with us can make all of the difference and infuse courage into any new exploration.

Tracy knew that her group would come for her because she knew if roles were reversed she would come back for them. The simple and powerful connection we make with people that share common values and cause is and has always been the key to discovery. Once we figure out that we don't have to be self-reliant and learn to trust in our "buddy" the world presents options that we could never consider before.

It's still a new year filled with possibilities. Find a friend and start climbing.

Szenippet: With love in our heart we never travel alone.

■ ■ ■

Silent Sequel
A Sixty-Word SZEN Story:

It had been a couple of years since the book had been pub-lished, and Charlene knew that it was time to write the sequel. She had promised her readers an "end to the story" and now wondered if she was willing to share what really happened. If she told the truth she would be vulnerable, but if she didn't she'd be lost forever.

And more…
I think there are new chapters and sequels in our lives that we sometimes fail to examine closely. Growing and maturing sets us on a path and through a gauntlet of sorts that provides experience, both love and pain, and for sure, nets out a great deal of wisdom. As life progresses, the rules and sometimes the people and places change. And whether we recognize it or not, we're not the same person we were when we started our journey.

When we turn over a chapter in our lives, we're not always aware that anything has really changed. Yet if we study what is in the rearview mirror, we often will see a landscape that looks nothing like the road ahead. The road ahead features the one thing that the past can't foresee with certainty and that's the unknown. Along our path are new places, people and situa-tions to be embraced or avoided. And each place or person we encounter has the potential to become a major player in this next season of our lives.

As authors of our own story, we can either head in the same circular direction - meeting the tried and true along the way and enjoying the predictability of it all - or we can veer onto a new road where anything can happen. Whatever we choose, we still are growing and both paths offer opportunity to explore; both represent a plot twist to our story. We can either see the same things with new eyes, thereby discovering what we've been missing, or we can shift our view to vistas we've never seen. Both can fill us up with joy. And at the core of that joy lies truth, and like Charlene, we'd all be lost without it.

Szenippet: Our hearts must cross the bridge between what is and what could be first, and then the rest of us will follow.

■ ■ ■

CHAPTER 2

The Productivity Promise

Tips for making internal changes, using your time better and increasing your energy

CHAPTER TWO EDITOR'S NOTES – A PREVIEW

Free Time (making the most of your free time)

Sunday Serenity (take time to rest and renew and you will be stronger)

Flashpoint (What looking for your path, make sure you are looking in the right place, repeat flashlight analogy)

Monday Moaning (how to use your weekend well)

Waitless (using time more productively, and not waiting around for things to happen.)

3 Steps to Positive Change

A Time for Us (using the minutes in between productively)

The Art of Closure (find ways to get closure, even in the middle of projects)

Mantra Makeover** (develop a mantra to help reach your goals)

Rebootability (reboot your brain to give yourself a fresh start)

Detachment dividends (detach from the outcome)

Your Move (take action Ben Franklin analogy)

Choose Not Lose (let go of the old, and set yourself free)

Change for Life (don't get stuck in routines, find ways to change.)

Free Time

From the Szenabling file:

Having free time means that for some reason we have been given an allotment of time that is ours to spend as we choose. The concept of *free time* means that there is nothing scheduled to get in the way of doing something that is unscheduled. We've all heard people say: "Sure when I get some *free time*, I'll come by and fix the whatever." Or, "If I had a little more *free time* I could finish that project, go on that trip, catch up on my sleep etc." *Free time* is so valuable that we have elected to consciously not give it a price. We call it free even though we know there is a price somewhere in there in the fine print of our mind's rationalization process.

Time is fascinating. It can make us feel good or bad depending on the context. Work time usually isn't as much fun as playtime. Commute time seems to steal time away from quality time which only exists in whatever moment we think is quality for us. Time, as Einstein proclaims, is relative and it is there for all to use in any way we choose. The late Steve Jobs on the subject of spending time wisely said: "I have looked in the mirror every morning and asked myself: If today were the last day of my life, would I want to do what I am about to do today? And whenever the answer has been "No" for too many days in a row, I know I need to change something."

We all commit time, invest it, waste it and eventually run out of it. Throughout all of our time, time remains a constant companion. Time doesn't judge us. It lets us use as much or as little on whatever we see fit. And this will never change; time is "free", which in its essence is why it's so valuable. If we had to pay for the time we use we'd be more careful about what we use it for. But because it's free, we sometimes think we can always get more.

This last weekend we reverted back from Daylight Savings Time to Standard Time (is that daylight losing time?). An extra hour was given back to us. I'm not sure how you might deal with having an extra hour, but I like to relish the concept and purposely don't set the clock to the right time before I retire. That way when I awake and look at the clock and it says 8:00, I know it's really only 7:00 and wow does that seem like a real bonus – a whole extra hour! What if, however, during the night there was a power outage and the electricity was out for two hours. So waking up and looking at the 8:00 time would mean that it's not really 7:00 but actually 9:00. It happened: the extra free hour was sucked up into the vortex of the netherworld and I was penalized an hour for no apparent reason. So instead of having time to catch up, I'm already behind. To alleviate the stress of not being able to thoroughly enjoy an extra hour I've decided to start the Book of Szen a bit earlier today. This helps me regain control of my schedule and by finishing an hour earlier, I will have saved an hour, which I can spend later.

The hands of time are restless and relentless so to truly enjoy the hour saved, we have to move it into the *free time* allocation category. Once it's there we can spend it any way we choose. Having more free time is having more time to live, because we've recognized the clock in ourselves. We all have our own internal clock, and it alone sets the pace and the value of the minutes of our lives. Every minute counts even when it's free.

Szenippet: All time is free until we decide otherwise.

■ ■ ■

Sunday Serenity
A Sixty-Word SZEN Story:

Becky had been working long hours for the whole week. She needed to relax. When Sunday arrived she contemplated how not to do "anything," - no work, interaction or thoughts (if that was possible). All she wanted was peace. She sat back, put on the headphones and closed her eyes. The music was soft and she smiled - adrift and alone.

And more...
Shutting out the noise and the thoughts that connect to obligations, unfinished tasks and unsolved problems is necessary for survival. We all need to replenish and rejuvenate. By controlling the input, we can create an environment of peace and serenity. From walks alone and quiet drives in the country to headphones and yoga, there are plenty of options for shutting down and letting some tranquility in.

Being at rest and at peace lets the mind become quiet and gives us a chance to sort things out and gain some perspective on the myriad aspects of our life. There is something we each like to do that "calls" to us because of its replenishing power. For Becky it was music and for whatever yours might be, I hope you find time to add it to your life.

For me, it's writing. Thanks for letting me share what brings me joy.

Szenippet: In need of a respite from the crunch of life's stress, seek a place where you can go and just be - a place where you are loved for who you are.

■ ■ ■

Flash Point
From the Now & Szen file:

You can have the most powerful and strongest flashlight in the world, but if you're in the wrong cave you won't find a thing. Until we know what we're looking for, nothing else can happen. No answers can be found, no solutions will arrive and no peace can join us on the journey, unless or until we know where we're headed and why – "You can't get what you want, until you know what you want" - to quote a song.

In this context life is so very simple. All we have to do is imagine what we want for our lives and then move toward it. What happens sometimes though is we invest in getting the latest flashlight and go exploring in the wrong places. It becomes a frustrating adventure, like putting in the wrong GPS coordinates and wondering why we're not where we wanted to be. The trip offers no closure or reconciliation and never seems to satisfy. It's not that we're doing it wrong, it's that we're not looking toward the right spot to find our heart's calling. The flashlight salesman can tell use how to use it, but not what to shine it on. That's our job and that journey begins within.

However we may evaluate what we truly desire, we all need to have one of those "aha" moments – light bulb goes off, spontaneous awakening, epiphany or whatever else you want to call it, that becomes the flash point for our next chapter. From there our vantage point improves because now we know what we seek. And once we know that, we know where to seek it. Right cave, right light –bingo!

Szenippet: The wink of a single thought holds the power to illuminate our path. One single, elegant, clear-minded thought is all we need to change our world.

■ ■ ■

Monday Moaning
From the Szenabling file:

The weekend is the time to catch up on all of the errands and chores that can only be done when we have some time to do them. The weekend usually begins on Friday evening and ends Monday morning. In between, there are a limited number of daylight hours and a corresponding unlimited list of things to accomplish. The challenge is to get as many things off of the "to-do list" and still squeeze some time in for relaxing and recuperating. The list typically includes fixing, improving, cleaning, and moving things, plus attending family functions and events and maybe chauffeur your kids or parents somewhere..

Weekends tend to fill up fast. It's the time we plan for, work around, and think about during the rest of the week.

Sometimes we only live one weekend to the next, while the workweek in between becomes a rote passing of time. This is not to say that the workweek isn't filled with challenge and excitement, it's just that when we're working, time seems to drag a bit, and we often can't control our schedule like we can on the weekends. By default, "weekend's rule!" has become the mantra for modern man because we have some control and we can choose how we spend it.

On a good weekend, the weather is great, the to-do list is completed and there is time left to enjoy, relax and decompress. When you have a good weekend, the workweek ahead seems manageable. When the weekend doesn't go as planned, the undone and the unrest can take its toll. The traditional Sunday night setting of the alarm for Monday looms like an anchor on our psyche. When we awake on Monday, we awake not only to the week's agenda, but also to the unnerving tug on our system that reminds us that once again we have a whole week standing in the way of our cherished weekend. Here are a couple of ideas for putting Monday in a little better perspective:

- Call in sick – works like a charm.
- Prepare for Monday on Friday. Before you leave work on Friday, write a note to yourself and leave it at work to be read on Monday. The note includes a list of what you expect to accomplish over the weekend, including rest and relaxation. On Monday when you review your list, rate the enjoyment you derived from each task completed. The exercise will help you make a better, longer or shorter list for the next weekend. Remember though, to keep your list handy throughout the week because you might want to add something or even

better, you might find time during the week to take some things off the list.

- Always plan on doing at least one thing just for you. It should be the highest rated activity on your list (see above).
- Finally, every Monday challenge yourself to find joy in an unexpected place. Make it a priority and the next thing you know, it'll be Tuesday.

Have a great week, no moaning allowed.

Szenippet: If we treated vacations like we do work, they would last a lot longer.

■ ■ ■

Waitless
From the Szenabling File:

Have you ever thought about the amount of time that we spend waiting? The time we spend waiting for things like a plane, a phone call, a return text or an upcoming event like a graduation or wedding can really add up. Where did all of that time spent waiting go? How much was wasted on meaningless activities designed to help us pass the time so that we could get to that future moment? What if we had all of that time returned to us? What then?

Unfortunately there is no pause button in life. Unlike a TIVO setting, our lives can't be stopped and then restarted on demand. Whether we're wasting time or spending it wisely, time is not waiting for us.

In certain philosophies like Tao and Zen, there is no wait-ing, because this moment is all there is. Being in the moment is being free of the need to wait for anything. It's all already here, now; we're really all "Waitless". So the question is, now that we know that we can't stop time, how do we plan on using the time we have?

There is a trick to all of this, and it has to do with how we think and our own individual perspectives. It seems that our mind has known all along that it has the power to change our lives with a single thought. The amazing thing is that we get to choose that thought. And when our thinking is clear in sync with our values and goals we're rewarded with glorious moments where we feel so alive that it seems that time actually does stop.

So how do we create more of those *being alive* moments? Here are some thoughts:

Meditate: Just take a few moments and breath in and out slowly. Clear your mind of everything. This is how eastern reli-gions clear their mind of future and past and keep the "mon-key mind" at bay. Just concentrating on your breath teaches you how to stay present.

Take notice: If we can change our thinking to a new reality that states, "there is no down time, or waiting" we can free up those moments to dwell and visualize on our desired des-tiny. Regardless of whatever else may be going on in our lives, there is always enough mind space and time to hold a dream. And dreams can trump worry, which is a whole other chapter on what keeps us from enjoying the moment.

Take action: The best and maybe only way to create what we want is to know what we want and then move toward it. Do something. A small step, a note, a call, anything that gets us closer is good. A good way to start is to do research on the

Internet for the words that you have identified are related to your vision.

Live now: Leave the vision switch on when it comes to daily encounters with other things. It helps us stay in a self-empowered mode and it becomes easier to stay focused and not so stymied by the pull of the outside world. And over time, you may discover that the world is also influenced by our thoughts as well. It's all in how we see it that matters. And that individual, unique, self-realized view that is ours alone is created from the "Waitless" world we live in - the here and the now.

Szenippet: Whatever happens to you, it's what you do with it that counts.

■ ■ ■

3 Steps to Positive Change

This is just not working. I'm not making any progress and I can't seem to figure out what to do. I've been stuck in the same place for so long that I've become numb and worse yet, I've become so predictable that everyone I talk to can finish my sentences. I don't think this is really what I signed up for when I joined the human race. It surely can't be my destiny. Is this all there is?

The short answer is no. There is more, lots more. Here are some steps on how to find it, whatever "it" may be for you.

1. Before anything becomes real it has to be imagined. So by looking at what currently is real, all we can see is the result of our previous thoughts and imagination. Close your eyes to what is and dream of what if.

2. New dreams create new realities. If our "what if" dreams are ever going to come to fruition we have to be able to identify what that will feel like when it ultimately happens. Not the place we'll be standing or the people we'll be with, nor any other physical details, just the emotion that bubbles to the top - the one that causes a shout and a fist pump of joy, "YES!"

3. Repeat # 2 a lot. Frequency creates coincidence. When we hone in and focus on an end result that generates the joy we seek, we automatically begin to move toward the goal. That first step, whatever it may be, begins to draw events and circumstances to us that we need. Focus takes the "if" out of the "what if" and sure enough, what seems to be a series of coincidences eventually adds up to the "YES!" we've been seeking.

Positive change driven by imagination and not the details of getting there puts joy back into the journey - just like it's supposed to be. Enjoy yours.

Szenippet: If you don't know where to start, begin with how you want to end.

■ ■ ■

A Time for Us
From the Make Shift File:

Some time ago, while I was working as a DJ on a local radio station I learned about the value of time. When I first started, I was reluctant to leave the studio booth while a record was playing because I felt that the 2 or 3 minutes playing time was not enough to really do anything and that I might miss getting the next record on. However, after a short time observing the other DJ's, I recognized that a lot of things could be crammed into a few short minutes.

Eventually I got to where I could run down the hall, get a coffee, go to the bathroom, have a chat with the program director, and still have mega seconds left to cue up the next song and provide the announcer segue without losing my breath or a beat. Sometimes when I was working alone on the night shift, I would put on a tape with a few songs and actually leave the building to go get dinner. I developed a sense of calmness about seconds ticking by and knew that I could always squeeze out the time I needed.

Today, I'm still mindful of the multitasking options that only require seconds to enact. I think we all have the ability to use time efficiently and get things done while doing something else. It's like having a phone call while we're texting and sending emails or doing chores or something we can accomplish without really being present.

But what if we changed from simply using the time to investing the time? I mean taking some moments to make a difference for you and for those around you. If we think in terms of effectiveness instead of efficiency we move from a life that is process orientated to one that is goal-focused.

In this state of mind we can invest free moments in working on our vision for ourselves, reaching out with a smile or hello to those we meet or simply paying more attention to the person on phone. Just a couple of times a day to be present and soak up the moment keeps us connected and can rejuvenate our thinking.

The problem with multi-tasking is that it creates separation and reduces focus. We end up going through the motions, and at the end of the day we have moved things around and accomplished a bunch. Sometimes. however we forget to move our own cause and goals forward. If we could manage our life's dreams like we do a normal day's work and spend the same energy on reaching new goals, we'd get what we want. It only takes a few moments in between all of the hours we have everyday to make it happen. Spend a couple of moments for yourself and see what happens.

Szenippet: Time waits for no man is true, but it only takes a second to catch up.

■ ■ ■

The Art of Closure
A Sixty-Word SZEN Story:

Bill looked around the room. Papers were piled high on the desk, files were on the floor and a few random sheets of paper found their way to the carpet, silently resting, waiting for their fate to be revealed. Bill was feeling panicky. The volume of paperwork had stymied his progress. He felt choked, but knew he had to act.

And more...
Ever been buried with work or a long list of things to do and just felt immobilized with angst, not knowing where to start? Me neither, not since I've learned the art of closure. Practicing closure can help maintain balance and curb the insanity that

GARY D SZENDERSKI

comes with jobs and projects and "things to do" that never seem to get completed - You know, those things where the status is always "pending" some type of action or response or something else that has to happen first and they just don't seem to end. They linger like the pile in Bill's office and they also occupy brain cells and space in our memory banks.

Closure can help. It's a sense of finality that removes something from our list that doesn't return. It's the end of a project, the reconciliation of an agreement or the purging of the irrelevant and unnecessary from our psyche. It's freedom to move on to something new. It's the key to the cycle of life. Closure is popular as a New Year's resolution because it cleans up the loose ends and let's us move on. Here are a few ideas on how to integrate the art of closure into our routine:

- Know what's pending. Make a list of ALL that needs to done. Don't skip anything.
- Separate the list into things for us to do for ourselves and things to do for all others.
- On the list for all others, pick the easiest and get them done and cross them off the list – Anything we say we'll do, we should probably see it through.
- On the list that is for us, get out the red pencil and cross off everything that is pending an action by another because waiting for someone else to do something first is like waiting and worrying about the bus coming. Assume it will and get it off the list for now. Then delete everything that doesn't really matter and that no one will know if you do it or not. You can always add things back later but for now enjoy the peace of a short and more manageable list.

Closure creates a feeling of accomplishment. It adds the period that we all need to get on to the next thought. Now you can officially cross the reading of the Book of Szen off your list for this week. Doesn't that feel good?

Szenippet: No thought is ever complete until it comes to life.

■ ■ ■

Mantra Makeover

A broad definition of mantra is it is an expression, a few choice words or sometimes a sound that when repeated over and over creates positive vibrations that allow one to feel the calmness and peace of a meditative state. We all have employed mantras to help us concentrate, or remind us of a particular goal we may have, or to build internal self-confidence and a positive attitude that we'll be able to succeed at a specific task. The only true value of a mantra however is found in the experience, which it ultimately creates; in other words, if it's working great, if not, find or create another. Here are a few ideas:

- Start with the end in mind. Make your secret goal an integral part of your mantra.
- Include a strong attribute you possess or want to possess. For example "my self-confidence insures I'll achieve my ____."
- Make it easy to remember, make it rhyme, or put it to music. Humming a mantra also sends a positive vibration.
- Repeat as needed until your mojo returns. A successful mantra can create a superstar mojo.

- Take all of the credit for however its changed your life. After all, it all came from you in the first place.

Szenippet: The best mantra is the one that connects your faith to your true desire. Find it and you'll never be lost.

■ ■ ■

Rebootability

When our computer gets a bit clogged up with too many files open, trying to compute or upload too many things simultaneously, the response time to our key stroke commands slows to a crawl and we have to stop and reboot. The process lets our computer stop for a moment so it can catch up. It recalibrates and reorganizes so it can get back to its normal high efficiency self.

Same thing works for us. Try it. When things get so piled up that nothing seems to be getting done, that's the time to do nothing. We all need to reboot from time to time - to unplug for a bit, unwind for a while, and under achieve for a moment. To find a place in the mind that's not turning so quickly and linger there for a spell; a place where we get a chance to refresh. A place we can visit anytime we choose; all we have to do is hit restart.

Szenippet: Mini mental vacations are often the best trips we can take.

■ ■ ■

Detachment Dividends

When we hold on too much, and attach ourselves to an exclusive outcome that is out of our control, we miss the possibilities that cool detachment can offer. Only by relaxing our grip on what the future may bring can we attract what we truly desire.

Szenippet: The best dreams to come true are the ones we thought could never happen.

■ ■ ■

Your Move

From the Now & Szen file:

"All humanity is divided into three classes: Those who are immovable, those who are moveable, and those who move!" This wisdom comes to us courtesy of Benjamin Franklin. I like the way Mr. Franklin kept things simple and poignant and direct. That's why so many of his quotes and insights survive centuries and generations. His human centric observations remind us that as a species we may not have evolved as fast or as well as the technology and the 21st century life style that we now enjoy. Yes it's true that everything seems to be instantaneous and attainable, and although we all move so quickly, it's often on impulse. Thus in terms of our inescapable human nature, Mr. Franklin's quip, "haste makes waste" is truer than ever.

Both of the quotes noted here underscore my last week or so. The concept of moving and taking action is a simple notion, but it's amazing how often we are stymied and frozen with indecision. We may start as immovable and just dig in to resist change, and maybe graduate to moveable meaning that we are at least considering a change, but joining the ranks of actually moving, well that's another thing altogether. Taking action, moving toward a goal, sometimes kicks up some dust and sets events and circumstances into motion. Often the simple decision of actually moving draws what we seek closer to us.

A case in point is the trip I'm about to take to New York. It started as an opportunity to transform a long-time business acquaintance into a partnership. I had only a moment to decide whether to make the trip or not. I chose yes and am hopeful it will turn out well. There are some risks, or maybe better said, an investment to be made in meeting these folks from the UK. They can be difficult to nail down. To quote their leader: "We're still tying down our itinerary - it's like a tarp flapping in a hurricane."

To help me navigate the tentative nature of the business portion of the trip, I was fortunately able to include my son Adam and now the visit is much more of an adventure/vacation and has become a no lose scenario. Once I knew that Adam would be joining me, I booked everything as quickly as I could, which is my usual way, and how Ben's second quote, *haste makes waste* came to be ringing in my ears. Long story short, I booked us into the wrong hotel and when I finally noticed my mistake, the hotel that I wanted to be in was full. I scrambled and did ultimately find something suitable, but wasted time and a few brain cells in the process. To quote Mr. Franklin: "Lost time is never found again." It's true and maybe one of the best calls to action for getting the most out of what time is left.

To get some return on our life's investment, I think we need to stay active in the process and consider joining that third class of humanity that actually moves. The need to "move" can present itself as a well thought out personal decision, or a reaction to outside circumstances. Either way, remember to take Mr. Franklin's advice and "Don't confuse motion with action."

Whatever our next move is, it could be the one that changes everything and as long as it moves us toward our dream, the trip will be worth it.

Szenippet: There is no trip insurance for life's journey.

■ ■ ■

Choose Not Lose
A Sixty-Word SZEN Story:
All of the movies and videos were organized by title and genre and all of the labels were facing out so he could easily find the film of the week. His collection was enormous and the Sunday evening film ritual was something he cherished – movie, popcorn, and delight. But this Sunday was different. He inserted the tape into the player. He hit play. Nothing happened. The VCR had died.

And more...
Sometimes things that we get pretty used to go away. The VCR, the rotary phone and the delicious lunch served in coach class. Or maybe it's the friends that move, relationships that fade or life that moves on. And whenever something is taken off of our shelf, there is a moment of searching and sometimes

of panic. Replacing what was with something new sounds easy enough, but its not always true. Seems that change can be difficult especially when what was working fine, at least in our view, is suddenly not an option.

How we face new choices often determines if the new choice will work at all. Option 1: If we're reluctant to have something new in our lives because it's different and we resist, there is a good chance that whatever it is won't work and thus we prove to ourselves that something new isn't necessarily better. Option 2: If we embrace what's new, we'll learn quickly to appreciate the improvement. Both of these options however have nothing to do with the object of change, but rather with our own perspective.

As the keepers of our own disposition and point of view we have the capability to judge, evaluate, endorse, reject or accept whatever we choose. So even if options are removed and things like VCRs, free television, cassette tapes, or even relationships and special people in our lives go away, we still get to choose how we feel about it. That's where the power of the human spirit lies. Our feelings about anything or anyone start with us. We choose, even if we lose.

Szenippet: If we didn't choose where we are, who did?

■ ■ ■

Change For Life
From the Szenabling file:

Don't you just love routines? You know the daily activities that make up so much of our life such as: regular and predictable events, words, actions, encounters, car trips, menu items, personal hygiene, telephone conversations, people on our speed dial, plus a million other things that we perform by rote and sometimes unconsciously every single day of our lives.

If we were to examine all of our normal daily routine we'd find that so often we simply go through the motions. We've got our patterns and habits well learned and easy to navigate. If we're not careful and mindful we can easily find ourselves on a type of autopilot for great expanses of time that can absorb so much of our life that we look up at the calendar and see that we seemed to have missed some things. Sometimes these things can add up to include relationships, career paths, physical health and a whole slew of personal growth opportunities. All because we tend to gravitate towards what we know and resist change. But change can be our friend; here are a few things to consider:

- Creating something new begins with thinking something new. To make any kind progress or growth we need to examine two criteria for growth: Direction and Process.
  Direction sets the goal and often this forces a change in the process to get there. If the direction remains valid, perhaps we then need to examine the "way" we are pursuing it, if we're looking for improvement.
- The "way" we go about our lives defines who we are. By examining our own predictable routines and habits we may see that simple adjustments could net incredible returns.
- Forced and conscious change of what is will yield a better view of what could be. To make any kind of

course correction we're forced to get our bearings and this enhances our ability to visualize.

- "Life is unpredictable" is not a concept to be feared. Surprises do happen in our life and if we're expecting them or better yet creating them, we'll be able to get that much more living in.

We all know the expression "time flies when you're having fun." Time can also "fly" if we're not paying attention. What does more life or living free of routine look like? It looks like something has changed; maybe it's time.

Szenippet: Change is how we know we're alive.

CHAPTER 3

The Past – Letting Go

EDITOR'S NOTES CHAPTER THREE

No Thanks (don't continue to do something if it makes you unhappy)

Beyond Belief (get rid of limiting beliefs)

When I'm Sorry Isn't Enough (when relationships are over and can't be repaired, let them go.)

The Back of the Closet (shed the old to find the new)

Peace by Piece (it takes too much energy to maintain a status, be yourself and don't worry about it.)

The Power of Now and Then (your experience can create great things, if you stay in the moment)

No Thanks

How could he tell his wife of over 50 years that he would prefer that they would not host the Thanksgiving Day dinner and festivities anymore? Dealing with the stress of visiting relatives and having a perfectionist in the kitchen that worried about every single detail had turned the holiday into an ordeal. He felt the pressure and very little holiday joy. He longed for the light-hearted days gone by.

Malcolm was 78 years old, and would often quip that he could pass for 75. He had been married to Bunny for over 50 years. Her real name was Agnes and she was nicknamed Bunny, not because she had good hops or bounced about, but because she had lots of babies. Bunny and Malcolm had 11 children, 17 grandchildren and 3 great-grandchildren and the only time everybody could get together was Thanksgiving. As the official family intro to the holiday season, it was something that Malcolm used to look forward to, but over the last few years his enthusiasm had begun to wane. It was a tradition that somehow had morphed into drudgery. So many kids and so much to do. Even though he loved to see the family, the stress of getting everything ready created so much tension in the house that secretly Malcolm wished that they could skip the holidays altogether. Bunny, even though she was stressed to the hilt, would never think about deferring her role as matriarch. Plus she knew that Malcolm would never let her off the hook; she did it for him and would not let him down. But inside she too sought the return of the light-heartedness that used to define them.

On Thanksgiving morning, Malcolm could hear Bunny in the kitchen muttering what sounded like obscenities at the green beans. The mound of beans sat there in the dish, naked because someone forgot to buy the mushroom soup that so nicely covers them. Emily, the housekeeper and official grocery shopper for the couple, forgot to get the soup. As Bunny searched the cupboard in vain for a forgotten can or a substitute, the veins in her neck started to pop out. She knew as everyone did, that there was no replacement for mushroom soup when it came to green bean casserole. Bunny called out to Malcolm and told him to get on his coat and go the store.

Malcolm exchanged glances between the beans and the scowl on Bunny's face and suggested that one of the kids bring a can of soup. But he knew it would throw off the timing, and he reasoned that he had no choice unless he wanted to see his wife blow a gasket –a behavior that she had introduced to the marriage a few years ago whenever things were not coming out perfectly. This change in attitude put a lot of pressure on Malcolm who was anything but perfect. In those imperfect situations, a trip to the store was a welcome respite. As he got into the car, he fantasized an escape scenario – no soup, dinner, guests or hassles, just a football game and maybe a beer or two.

At the store he panicked when he saw that they were out of mushroom soup. How could this be and what would he tell Bunny? When she picked up the phone and he told her the bad news, he heard some kind of slam, crash, bang and loud moan, then silence. A moment or two later, he heard a giggle, which grew to a loud and somewhat hysterical laugh. Bunny had lost it he thought until he heard her say, "Okay, no problem. I quit, this is the last time I do this. I'm sorry, I know how much this means to you." She added, "Get home, the game is just starting."

Dinner turned out great, nobody really missed the mushroom soup on the green beans and as the family held hands and prayed before dinner Malcolm announced that this was the last Thanksgiving they would host. When the family asked, "are you sure"? Malcolm and Bunny in unison responded, "no thanks."

Szenippet: Giving thanks is the best gift you can give.

■ ■ ■

Beyond Belief
From the Make Shift File:

A belief is an organized pattern of knowledge that an individual holds as true about his or her world. In the marketing classes I teach, we study a number of different aspects on consumer behavior and the implications of their beliefs on their buying decisions. In this world, perception is reality. And every attitude we carry is based on what we believe. And every decision and every step we take or do not take to reach our goals is based on what WE hold to be true.

Our world works from the inside out. This means that whatever notion we have about our world is filtered through our belief system, which is lodged in our deepest thoughts, feelings and experience. We see what we believe we should see. This of course reinforces what we believe. And so we achieve what makes sense to us in our own world and belief system. But what if we want to change that world? How can we change our beliefs?

The first thing to do is recognize which beliefs are limiting to us. If we pay attention, we can spot our limiting beliefs through clues. Words like *can't, shouldn't, couldn't, won't, never, not* and *impossible* can pop up when we're thinking of making a positive change. We get stuck on the reasons we can't instead of the joy of we can. When this happens hold on to that thought.

Examine these beliefs. Where did they come from? Are they really true? What if they are not true? If it's possible that something we believe isn't really true, it's just as possible that what we want to be true is believable. We always gravitate to the believable because we weren't born with three wishes or a magic wand. We tend to follow the same old patterns. So here's the trick. Always state your dreams in the context of "why not" not "how to."

For example....

Remember it's not "I'll believe it when I see it", it's "I'll see it when I believe it." If we move a step into what we really want to be true about ourselves, we will begin to see that truth come to life.

Szenippet: What's impossible only becomes possible with faith.

■ ■ ■

When "I'm Sorry" is Not Enough

Many years ago I had a very best friend. From the second grade through high school, college and beyond we were best buddies. I was even his best man at his wedding, but some time after the honeymoon, I stopped being his friend. I didn't want to, he did, and for unknown reasons, to this day, I have no idea why. I wrote and called and waited trying to reconcile *something* that must have happened between us. I can't remember what I might have done or said, but I'm pretty sure I did *something*; otherwise he would call me back.

Sometimes things happen and relationships change and we're not clear on exactly why, and saying "we're sorry" is just not enough. Our personal inclination may be to try and fix it. However, if we don't know the problem, it's hard to find the solution. Furthermore, this line of reasoning assumes that all problems seek their own reconciliation - they somehow should emerge for us to easily spot and fix or at least try to fix. What if we never get the chance?

When we have a situation, where the problem is elusive, we have to recognize that it may never be found or clear. It may be impossible to fix. When we hit this cul-de-sac, all we can do is turn and take another direction. It may be unsettling, but it's best to let it go. Good luck old friend.

Szenippet: Regrets happen because of the past and they only live in the present if we invite them.

■ ■ ■

The Back of the Closet
From the Make Shift File:

If you could change just one thing about your life at this very moment, what would it be? What's missing? What needs to be let go? What's your wish? Whatever your answer is, linger on that thought for a moment and imagine how that change or wish might impact your life. Got it? Now while holding that thought, name the three things that you would do next once your wish is achieved.

Write them down right now.

1.
2.
3.

Next, ask yourself if any of the three things you identified could be accomplished without the wish. If the answer is yes, then you don't need a wish, you just need a plan.

In mastering the changes in our lives we often need to take baby steps before we can run. Often what holds us back is the stuff we keep in our head and in the back of the closet, thinking that some day we'll need it, whatever it is. If we can take a serious look and what we're holding on to and make a move to let it go, it just might lighten the load for the real journey that we need to be on.

Szenippet: Living an authentic life is not just about being real; it's about being open.

■ ■ ■

Peace by Piece
From the Szenabling file:

The social mask we call the ego is just such a busy bee all of the time. The ego is constantly trying to keep things in order and under control by maintaining our relative place in society.. The ego is okay if we're advancing our personal brand and people are loving us, but just as easily can wreak havoc on our psyche when we're not living up to our own or the world's expectations. The fear of rejection and falling out of favor is a big motivator for the ego, and it will do whatever it takes to rid itself of the uneasiness caused by disfavor.

Trying to keep our relative status is a full time job that is ripe for failure from the get-go. That's because the maintaining of appearances to all of those we encounter over time requires that we control perceptions. The ego is only interested in what other people think. So imagine how hard it is to control so many other egos and their collective thinking. It's flat out impossible. We end up learning the hard way that we can't control much of anything or anybody. But learn we must, as this is the first essential piece to solving the puzzle of enlightenment – to let go.

When we shift our viewpoint from the limited and selfish perspective of the ego and go deeper inside, we discover that there is some space where we can unleash a wellspring of peace. Once we encounter this sense of calm and comfort, we wonder why in the world would we ever go back and let the ego run the show. And just as we're thinking that very thought, we've lost the moment and are suddenly worrying about some thing we're supposed to be doing. And that thought begets another and pretty soon we're miles from the peaceful trance we held only moments ago.

It's an ongoing struggle to be sure, but it can be won if we tackle it a piece at a time. In the interest of full disclosure, I should point out that I am still working on this, and have yet to reach complete Nirvana. That said here are a few ideas on attaining inner peace:

Let go. Rejection, resentment, loss of love, hurt feelings, damaged pride, you name it, these are the memories that hold us back. They are long gone and now just cumbersome and painful recollections of some place in time where our ego got beat up or bruised. It's over, time to move on.

Live now. Whatever is happening in our life today is here because of everything we've ever done before. We've arrived at the precise place and time we intended. We may not like where we are, but it doesn't matter. What matters is finding some way to carve out a simple space in our hearts to forgive and forget. Take a moment now to simply ponder this moment we're in.

Relax. Shut out the thinking and the noise and breath in the wonder of the glorious you within; always at ease and in peace.

Be yourself. A by-product of self-discovery is the unapologetic appreciation for the wonderful person you've become. Remember, the you inside is the only you that you need to be. You are incredible in every way, you are blessed, and you have so much love to give and share that you'll burst if you don't let it out. It's an unbelievable thrill to be the playful spirit and timeless adventurer that you are. Stay the course. We all love you.

Szenippet: You never have to apologize to anyone, not even yourself for your happiness. You earned it; it's yours.

■ ■ ■

The Power of Now & Then

I had lunch today with some very dear friends from another life. We were colleagues and were very successful in changing our part of the world. In the process we bonded, and although it was a couple of decades ago, it seemed like yesterday. We toasted friends and associates that are no longer with us, and we reminisced about the good and the bad. And then turned our attention to the present and what's next. It seems there will be an encore for the team (which is a much longer story) and it's not based on joining forces again because of skill sets or financing or who we know; it's based on trust. And with trust, any two people or group can accomplish anything. And so we will.

I share that story because in the world of encores and new chances there are insights, experience and knowledge from before that can be applied to the present, making the second time around an even more enjoyable journey.

■ ■ ■

I have often written about the power of being in the moment and appreciating what is happening this very second. Being in the now is empowering in many ways because it frees us from the burden of the past and worry of the future. Being present and aware allows us to gather more input and develop a greater ability to absorb what is happening now. Noticing details about surroundings or the look and words of people we're with is heightened when our mind stops living in the past or future and pays attention to what is right now.

It takes real practice to stay in the moment, but it's worth it. If we learn to use the now as a place of engagement or even refuge from worry, we begin to get a glimpse of ourselves observing ourselves. This self-observation and reflection is extremely useful when applying all of the previous moments of our life – the *then*– to what will be the *new now*. In other words, like my story at the top, our experience, good or bad, is always with us and available to help construct and hopefully enjoy the now that is currently upon us.

The power of "then" lies in its symbiotic relationship with our psyche and ego. Whatever we may have learned can be useful in any given moment. And any given meditative aware-ness of the moment, the power of now is the most fertile time for launching new thoughts and writing new chapters in our life. That's because whatever path we have taken to get to this place in time, has prepared us for the "new now" we're about to slide into. If we tap into what got us here, we can create a better version of ourselves from here forward, one step, one chapter, one moment at a time.

Szenippet: Good judgment requires experience and the best experience is often gained through bad judgment.

■ ■ ■

CHAPTER 4

Living in the Present

EDITOR'S NOTES CHAPTER FOUR

Got A Moment (use your moments well and they'll turn into a great life)

Becoming (become who you are, don't wait, repeat)

Just Follow the Signs (have a goal and pay attention, don't live on autopilot)

The Time That's Left (use the time that's left to you well)

Hold that Thought (as we enter new rooms, clear away the debris, and you will have breakthroughs.)

Catch And Release (enjoy the journey, even if you may have to start over - fishing analogy)

In the Dark (don't run away from the gift of love)

Spine Tingling (how to create positive change, using the acronym SPINE)

Ouija Bored (don't get stuck in the status quo. Find exciting and even scary options)

June in the Room (take advantage of your vacation)

Doors Open Now (crisis helps us focus and make changes)

Got a Moment
From the Make Shift File:

A moment is defined as an indefinitely short period of time, an instant. Some moments are meant to be, of truth or of the "ah ha" variety. We've all had our moments and some of them were defining while others were never dull. If asked to wait a moment we usually do, and often we need to shift with only a moment's notice.

Another definition of moment is that it is the *now*, the present. There are two versions of how the *now* arrives. Some moments that arrive are constructed of events and circumstance that are out of our control. That doesn't mean however that we need to be surprised. Often we have insights and instincts that give us clues as to how things may unfold. And when we're prepared for the possibilities we can create positive outcomes. When preparedness meets opportunity it's called good luck and that is often all we need to seize the moment.

The other version of the *now* occurs when we create and manage events to our own liking. In those moments we tend to relish exactly what is. In fact we want to be in the moment as long as we can. We like where we are, our space and place in time. We enjoy what we've created and life is just great. Some people can string these moments in time together into a lifetime of fulfillment.

The ability to manage moments is what creates momentum. Momentum is mass in motion and motion only occurs in the present, the *now*, a place where time stops. Time is the movement of thought. The past is memory and the future is imagination. The *now* is what really is and it's ours to enjoy as long as it lasts.

Szenippet: When we take for granted that there will be many more moments like these, we steal some of the wonder and the beauty of the moment we're in.

■ ■ ■

Becoming

Something truly great is about to happen. You can feel the tension and anxiety inside and you wonder if you are ready. Well, whether you're ready or not, it's coming soon and there is no way to stop it. So you might as well accept the greatness that lies within you, rise to the challenges ahead and take all of the good fortune you were meant to have.

The process of be-coming or the passing into another better season or chapter in our lives is something to be cherished. Don't doubt that you deserve it, you do. Your heart orchestrated everything you needed to get you to this point. Your heart was the inner voice that kept you going. The voice that encouraged you when things seemed hopeless. The voice that convinced you that it is your time to shine. The voice that speaks now of what's becoming. It's reminding you to embrace your destiny - you've earned it and it's yours for the taking. Remember, if you miss it and this chance passes you by, it may never return. And then, what will you become?

The choices we make about our own future are based on the options we create for ourselves. But no one option is ever completely certain and so there is always a risk of failure. The greater risk might be in not acting and assuming that there will be another chance, later. But waiting for the perfect time is an illusion. There is no perfect time, there is only this time, your best first chance. You know that you're as ready as you will ever become.

> *The only thing that separates the you today from the new and powerful you that's meant to be is the step that your heart is begging you to take.*
> **From the Book of Szen**

Szenippet: We may have chosen our path in life, but once on the path there will certainly be other interesting intersections; stay alert.

■ ■ ■

Just Follow the Signs
From the Make Shift file:

Have you ever had the experience of going to a particular place a number of times as a passenger, and then when asked to drive, you have no idea how to get there? The reason that we can shut out details about almost anything that happens around us, when it's not affecting us directly, is because we tune out what doesn't effect us directly.

Our mind and our thoughts decide what gets in and what doesn't. Of course there will always be some things that happen that will get our attention, but generally speaking, our world is of our own creation. We determine to what extent we need to pay attention and that's what we absorb.

We can, over time, set ourselves up to exist on autopilot. We've done the same thing so many times, that we think we already know what is happening or even going to happen, and thus we turn our attention and our thoughts elsewhere. This is what makes multi-tasking and daydreaming possible. The bad news is that while in this state we may be missing some pretty good stuff that might change our lives for the better.

Here are some thoughts on how to see what we might be missing:

Have a goal orientation – Setting goals, having a vision or a dream for something we want in life is the only way to get what we want. And when we have a clear goal in mind and the belief that we deserve to reach it, we shift from passenger to driver.

Pay attention - Attention generates an internal energy that allows us to create. Paying attention requires that we stay in the moment and it's in those moments where creativity reigns and destiny is formed.

Follow the signs - Once we're driving on our own, we begin to see the landscape change and we start to notice signs that point the way, and all we need to do is follow the signs. And we may find that we've been on the right path all along. Or perhaps it's time to make a shift. The good news is, we'll know.

Szenippet: For whatever journey we're on, it's okay to ask for directions.

Szenippet: Sometimes you can find happiness, but often it finds you.

■ ■ ■

The Time That's Left
From the Szenabling file:

We all know that time never waits, people do. We use time when we take time to explore options or are waiting for something or someone to "happen" to us, or maybe we're simply planning on how to use the time that hasn't arrived yet. We take time for everything. And time does not care one way or the other on how we use it. It only matters to us and it's strictly our perspective on whether or not it's being spent wisely. That's why Einstein was right about the law of relativity. He said "Put your hand on a hot stove for a minute and it seems like an hour. Sit with a pretty girl for an hour and it seems like a minute. That's relativity."

This correlates nicely to another axiom on time: "Time flies when you're having fun." This is because positive feelings and emotions propel us and negative ones slow us down. Therefore the simple secret to happiness is to have more fun and that's how positive people think. A pessimist however would counter with something like: "So I guess the more fun we have, the faster time goes and the sooner we run out of it." With that line of thinking pessimists prefer sadness and stress because they would argue the days drag so slowly and thus they are getting more time. Time to worry and fret about all of the bad things that might happen. It's all relative for sure, but it doesn't need to be so sad.

The point here is that the time that's left is all we have. It's all we have to give and to use and to hopefully enjoy. The neat thing is that we get to choose how we spend it and most importantly how we perceive how it's being spent - No one else, just us.

Time is a gift and eventually it will all be used. From right now until then, all that matters really is what we do with what's left. And what I just did was write this for you. It took about an hour, but seemed like a minute.

Szenippet: Time waits for no man, but he seems to wait for women.

■ ■ ■

Hold That Thought
From the Szenabling file:

Have you ever walked into a room and stopped at the doorway and thought to yourself that: You know you had a good reason for coming into this room, but somehow you can't seem to remember what. So then you look around the room for clues that might spark that elusive thought that brought you to the room to begin with. Eventually the thought works its way back to a conscious level and you remember.

What if on a grander scale we are constantly entering new rooms in our life that offer clues that will spark the essential thought that drew us there? And maybe they are not so much clues as memories left behind – Mental debris that's piled into the "living" room of our mind. In this room resides every thought we ever had: Every idea, every dream, and every fear.

This room holds secrets from the past as well as the kindling needed to change the future. It's all there within us waiting for our command. Whatever we want to think, or remember, or speculate begins with our will.

Sorting through the possibilities of "what's next" can be laborious. And sometimes we experience spontaneous inspiration – an idea that breaks through, and even though it may be tempered and restrained a bit by old thoughts, gains strength for its elegance and sense of purpose. An idea like that has the power to get us moving and thinking about what could be. The more we focus, the stronger it becomes until it dominates any thoughts or memories that could get in our way.

Armed with our ideal idea, our thoughts begin to conform to a new paradigm. Our mind sets the table for an expected feast and we draw energy and like-minded support to our cause. We literally begin to create our mind's eye vision, all because of a single thought. A thought that, at least for us, seemed attainable and real enough to actually happen. A thought held so tightly that it changed our world.

Now, why did I write this?

Szenippet: The first thing we need to believe in before a new chapter begins is that we have the power to really turn the page.

■ ■ ■

Catch & Release

A Sixty-Word SZEN Story:

Benjamin feared the future. He would take the largest por-
tions, save the most money, buy the biggest whatever but
then worry about what might happen to lose it all. No matter
how much he acquired, it was never enough; always too many
rainy days ahead to stop stockpiling. It felt safe and secure.
Then it rained, and he had to start over.

And more...
The concept of starting over from scratch is pretty common.
When a recipe goes awry, an investment goes south, or a relationship doesn't work out, we find ourselves having to begin
again and even change course. Beginning again from point
zero can not only be frustrating but also debilitating. That's
because we tend to focus on the time that was wasted to
attain whatever we lost, and we vow not to go down that same
path again. However, depending on our perspective, it might
be the only path we know.

Sometimes like in a recipe we can try something different
or just as easily retrace our steps and fix our mistakes. If it's
an investment lost, we might have to rethink a lifestyle, find
another investment to offset it or maybe reinvest because we
still believe it's the best route to take.

The same thing is true in relationships. The options for any
restart are similar: Hang on or let go, reinvest or divest, change
or stay the course. Whatever we choose, the end result will be
different each time anyway.

No journey is identical. What we have learned to get to this point changes the landscape moving forward even if we think we're repeating the same steps - The world moves, people change, perspectives vary. It rains. The terrain can be slippery, footing unsure and destiny unclear. The only thing that we know for sure is that nothing is for sure. We knew this, right?

It's the *not knowing* part of starting over that turns out to be the real gift. When we don't know something then we can't take it for granted. Not knowing keeps us in the present. And this helps us enjoy the process and not the destination. It's like fishing and loving the action on the line and the thrill of setting the hook. And if we use the right bait it's fun no matter what because it's not about the fish it's about the act of fishing. Catch and release is another way of saying enjoy the moment and then enjoy the next and the next, and the next etc. because they're all different.

Szenippet: The best fishermen are not just patient, they're attentive.

■ ■ ■

In the Dark
A Sixty-Word SZEN Story:

Just before the light went out and darkness filled the room, he noticed her robe slip from her shoulder and fall to the floor. He could hear the softness of the steps she took toward him. He thought on how many times he ran from those steps, but now, he was ready. He felt her touch and the darkness vanished...

And more...
So often we run from life's gifts. We reason we're not worthy or entitled or plead ignorance. Somehow though, love works her magic, and we see the light go on. Illumination and readiness come together and what was not, becomes what is. It's a beautiful crossing of the chasm of doubt into acceptance. That's where the light shines brightest and that's where love blooms.

Every seed of love needs nurturing to grow and to thrive. And for every seed of doubt uprooted, love's roots take a stronger hold. Every living creature needs to see the light to grow and in love. The light shines strongest when it illuminates the corners of doubt and fear. As it washes its brilliance across the din of the past, it leaves a spark of light for the next hopeful moment. In love, it's all about embracing the moments and our willingness to accept its gift and keep the light glowing.

...When he saw the robe fall to the floor it was a sign that what would happen next would change everything; there is always a clue to decipher when it comes to emerging from the dark. May your clues be obvious and fun to solve.

Szenippet: Being in the dark and not knowing keeps us from the knowledge we need to move. Once we move to the light, it streams its guiding glow, and the movement it embraces makes us fearless.

■ ■ ■

Spine Tingling
A Sixty-Word SZEN Story:

The "lock-down" cost her a whole class day with no way to make it up before graduation. She thought about scaling back the assignments and reading, but understood that in this course nothing could be skipped. Everything mattered and all the dots had to be connected. Like an elaborate recipe, how the ingredients interact to each other makes it unique.

And more...
Recently I was fortunate to be able to meet with some new people and some old friends to discuss how to create positive change in our lives. The source of the discussion was the Book of Szen and I was able to recite some of my favorite stories written over the last eight years. As I was preparing the workshop, I reviewed a number of different excerpts and re-discovered that there are 5 essential elements necessary to create positive change:

Self-exploration (discovery) – Diving into what we see and understand of ourselves is often the place where true change and a shift in our lives begin. Nothing really surpasses the power of self-discovery when it comes to understanding what's missing for us.

Perspective (wisdom) – Any newfound insights we may have are passed through our own filtering system. We carry all of our history and regardless of what anyone else may see or say, we alone know what we really believe.

Imagination (vision) – This is one of our greatest gifts and assets for creating a blessed life. Our thoughts on what if and what could be create a sort of internal goalpost when it comes to navigating change. Only after the vision is in focus can the journey begin.

Now (moments in time) – Much has been said and written about being in the now, that moment in time that simply "is." The now is not fleeting but a constant and allows us infinite time to assimilate and appreciate where we are and what we're feeling. All change happens in the now.

Energy (Drive) – Nothing at all happens without energy. It is what connects all of us together and to a constantly moving universe that can be persuaded to follow our commands. Energy creates movement and outcomes, invites serendipity, and generally makes miracles happen.

The five essential elements for creating positive change, like the acronym it spells, S.P.I.N.E., control and coordinates our nervous system and every living aspect that allows us to adapt, and enjoy our unique human power to create and make things happen. SPINE also refers to *character* and serves as a reminder that any of us, or all of us, possess the insights and tools to take emerging dots and connect them in magical ways - to get from wherever we are, to exactly where we want to be.

Szenippet: A tingling in our spine can be a sign of a journey about to begin where new dots emerge and connect in miraculous fashion.

■ ■ ■

Ouija Bored
A Sixty-Word SZEN Story:

The ages ranged from 4 to 12. There were two girls, the oldest and the youngest and two boys. They poured over the books, games and various toys that were for sale and laid out in irregular rows covering the entire driveway. Garage sales became an invitation and excuse for the children to explore. And this time they found themselves.

And more…
As we get older we often become so familiar with a routine or a relationship that we forget that change is still in play. Not just change of the people in our life but also inside change to ourselves that's been taking place so silently all along that we've failed to notice just how different we've become. When we finally realize that we're not the same person we thought we were, it can often be a shock to the status quo and reveal a richer, deeper, smarter and wiser person than we give ourselves credit for.

This occurs throughout our life because our learning curves, due to our experience, get shortened. We grasp things more quickly, and over time we can take the whole of all of the facts, happenings and events in our life for granted. New stuff keeps coming in, and yet we often assume that nothing new is happening inside. But of course it is. We evolve. We grow. We know. And this cycle of adding in what's new is actually easier to assimilate the older we become.

I understand that some might say that age creates nothing but habits that we cherish as indications that we're in control. They say we become reliant on habit and are reluctant to change. I disagree. I know that the concept of "the best is yet to come" is actually a truism and happens every day when we remain open to the possibilities. It's the openness that keeps us fresh. It's letting what's new and different find a place in our older self just like it did when we were younger. And once we approach each new day with awareness of what we're really attracting in our lives, the sooner we can appreciate the magic of living. It's like finding a Ouija board at a garage sale. We can, just like children, ask whatever we want and not be afraid of the answers. As time moves on, self-discovery becomes an asset, and it guarantees that we'll never get bored playing the game.

Szenippet: A better version of ourselves awaits to be awakened and anxious to fly. And take off can happen any moment.

■ ■ ■

June in the Room
A Sixty-Word SZEN Story:

"What are you staring at Riley?" The question broke the silence and the wave of calm that Riley was feeling. He was looking out the window of the 3rd floor of the school library, fixated on summer vacation and the sheer joy of leaving all of the books that now surrounded him. "Nothing much," he said. "Just contemplating my options."

And more...

Sometimes the season on the outside is in alignment with our own personal season inside. The weather calls and the heart responds. With summer just around the corner, change is in the air calling for a break in the action for anybody that has the time and disposition to take advantage of the age-old concept of "vacation." It's billed as the yearly, relaxing break from the routine. It can be a time for rejuvenation, exploration or self-discovery and sometimes all three.

We're not sure where Riley's mind has taken him, but it's probably not anyplace close, literally or figuratively, to where he is now. Vacations tend to take us away because it's the distance that provides the all-important perspective. Away from home we see things differently. Away from routine we see change. Away from commitment we see opportunity.

What about this June? It's a good bet that the concept of vacation and summer has already arrived in whatever room we're in right now. It's probably visited that room in our minds many times before the date actually arrived. So what are we waiting for? Let's take advantage of the season and our disposition, like Riley, to explore the options.

In order to determine which option is right for us, we simply play it out in our mind and if it generates a broad relaxing smile simply thinking about it, that's the one. May your reality surpass your dream.

Szenippet: We really don't take time off on vacation; we simply reapply the time we have to something we *want* to do, not *have* to do.

■ ■ ■

Doors Now Open
A Sixty-Word SZEN Story:

Steve felt weak. He was slipping away, knowing that this passing was only a door, but he hesitated to enter. He heard voices all around shouting words that he couldn't understand. One word pierced his cloud of confusion: "CLEAR!" The jolt lifted him off the table and in that brief millisecond he returned. And the door remained closed for now.

And more...
Sometimes a situation or even a crisis falls upon us that redefines our future. A moment arrives when we're able to get a glimpse into our own psyche to see who we really are. The clothes and title and all of the external aspects of our identity suddenly seem completely irrelevant. Miraculously we're able to perceive not just what is, but what could be. And in that moment of perception emerges the self-designed embryo of our alter ego – a different version of ourselves that is waiting for us to get out of its way.

Life has a way of accelerating that inhibits us from seeing the landscapes and relationships we may be passing by. The blur of living draws us into repetitive and predictable patterns that eventually become rote. The uneventful result is where we are now. It's our safe haven and control central dashboard from where next steps and our own evolution is predetermined and set in motion.

As we spy the possibilities for the future we have the choice of changing course or changing ourselves or both. Here are a few thoughts on the options:

- Changing course takes who we are and moves us to a different place, opportunity, challenge or story. Our essential character is all that remains.
- Changing ourselves requires we modify our perspective, patterns and self-awareness in a way that takes current happenings and turns them into our favor. We change the story from within.
- Changing both the course and ourselves is exciting but drastic and not recommended because the results will be harder to trace back and understand which one created the outcome.

Like Steve, we may face doors that suddenly emerge and can be life changing. But there are other doors too that we can move toward that open to new possibilities within - where we get to pick and can lead to self-fulfilling prophecies that transform the blur of living into a creation of our own choosing. Doors now open.

Szenippet: When one confronts routine, our view of life expands. Doors open wide and joy flows within.

■ ■ ■

CHAPTER 5

Creating the Future

EDITOR'S NOTES CHAPTER FIVE

The Unseen Vision (don't plan too much, if you want to be surprised with the result.)

Chapter Too (go inside to figure out the next steps)

The Road Ahead (follow your dreams, Yogi Berra analogy)

The One Step Process (set your goals, and focus on them)

Straight On Till Morning (look to what's next and don't get stuck in ruts - from Peter Pan)

Sow What (accept outcomes and be happy with results.)

The Unseen Vision
A Sixty-Word SZEN Story:

The picture hook was all that was left hanging over the fireplace. The shaded lines still visible against the faded paint indicated that what was there nearly filled the entire space rising to the 12-foot high ceiling. He imagined that it was glorious and commanded attention, praise and awe. He then carefully removed the hook, and painted over its past.

And more...
The danger in planning a trip too thoroughly and carefully is that once we finally arrive at our destination, we only see

exactly what we expected to see. We gravitate to the sights, events and venues that we thoughtfully charted in advance. The result is that the pictures we take match the ones in the tour guide and we deem the trip a success.

The same can be said for how we live our lives. We start with a menu of choices and options along with many helpful opinions, and we fill in our days and nights checking off the milestones and piling up memories that create our own personal tapestry. When we plan, we create expectations and so often what we envision comes to be. It's quite an elegant and sophisticated formula for living – Have a vision and move toward it.

What happens though when we've been there and done that too often? What if we go to the same job, spa, club, restaurants, resorts and events so often and predictably that, over time, instead of exciting us, we begin to grow bored? What then? What next? The answer is whatever.

As thinkers we have a distinct advantage and when we grow restless and are turning a page in our lives we can often see the choices fulfilled in our minds even before we move toward them. We can become so adept at imagining that we can play out nearly any scenario we desire, the good and the bad, in a mental preview mode. We begin to literally experience our future, head first, in thoughts before actions. So it's up to us what strokes we place on the canvas of our minds and what work of art we'll complete for all to see. We are all masters in the art of our life and we can turn what's been inside and unseen into our own original masterpiece.

Szenippet: Planning is great, but it doesn't help if your goal is to be surprised and excited with new possibilities.

■ ■ ■

Chapter Too
From the Make Shift File:

No one who has ever achieved his or her dream has stopped there. Getting what we want tends to encourage us to want more. So we strive to go to the next level, to raise the bar and reach greater heights.

The opposite is true when we cannot reach our goal. We tend to revaluate and rather than fail, reduce the dream to something a bit more attainable. The common denominator for either outcome is our internal driving mechanism that allows us to either raise or to lower the target. It's been called many things...desire, willpower and/or drive. Whatever we call it, we need to have it to make things happen.

We are an incredibly flexible species and have an amazing ability to switch gears, change direction and rationalize the appropriate perspective in an instant. We sometimes take this power for granted and forget that what we envision for ourselves is usually what we receive. If we examine our current chapter in life, we'll see that all of the choices, non-choices and energy we brought to bear have served to get us to where we are now. So at this point of the story, it's a good time to bookmark it and reflect a little and consider chapter too.

Chapter Too means there is more to go, to see, to have. There is more to love. There is more to dream. And the key to writing this next chapter, the way we want it, is to harness the very same energy and self-image that got us this far and use it to reach something farther or different. The power to activate Chapter Too resides within us and only needs a clear peek at the goal to get the wheels turning. See the goal, anticipate the feeling of reaching it and let that feeling spark our actions.

Like moving toward a sound, the feeling will grow as we move toward the source. As we revise the script, the new page will write itself and just as sure as we got to now, we can get to there too.

Szenippet: Outside forces can influence the speed of achievement, but the degree of achievement is up to us.

Writing our life story is more exciting when we get to choose the perfect ending.

■ ■ ■

The Road Ahead
From the Now & Szen file:

America's beloved philosopher Yogi Berra had some great advice on how to find our way. He said: "When you come to a fork in the road, take it." This is truly misspoken genius and can really be helpful as a guide when we face choices and change in our lives. Often when we do come to a roadblock or face unclear options, there is a temptation to hover and speculate for a long time on which might be the right path to take. For Yogi, the answer is simple, keep moving. Our answer for when we get stuck might be a bit more deliberate and complicated, but there is wisdom in the notion of taking action.

What supports the idea of *keep moving* is that the world has changed so dramatically in terms of speed connections. We have and access to information never before available, and new opportunities both personally and professionally are bubbling up everywhere.

Renaissance creates new layers of potential and dispels the notions of a direct path or a single straight line to our dreams. Now more than any time ever on this planet we find ourselves in a driver's seat of epic proportions. For example, the computing power of the smart phone we have in our pocket is more than all of NASA had in 1969 to put a man on the moon.

Today's world and the options we have to consider could be daunting if we don't know where we want to go, but for those with a destination in mind, it's truly liberating. And the good news too is that we have a built-in mechanism to cope with all of this newfound data and noise in that we tend to see only what we look for, and miss the rest. This means that when focused, our minds only attract and are drawn to what we want and expect to find. So even if we take a wrong turn or are knocked off of our path we'll still be able to navigate and get back in the right direction. What happens is our dreams act as the coordinates and our minds function as the GPS. Once we get the heading right, we can be blown off course, get stalled, or encounter a storm, but we still have the means to get there, wherever there might be.

With power like this, why wait even another second to set the course; the road ahead awaits. Get packed, it's time to meet your future and as Yogi also said: "The future ain't what it used to be." See you there.

Szenippet: It doesn't matter which path we take as long as we know where we're going.

■ ■ ■

The One Step Process
From the Szenabling file:

There are two types of people: goal oriented and process oriented. For the world to operate effectively we need both. And as different as each type is, they can learn a lot from each other. Having a goal orientation is about recognizing the opportunities and clearly seeing the possibilities for achievement. A process orientation means understanding that things just don't manufacturer themselves out of thin air, we have to have a plan.

Individually, we share a little of each orientation: The part of us that sees and sets the goals, and the part that finds a way to achieve them. A simple example would be taking a trip. First we decide where we want to go and next we determine the best means to get there. The more distant the destination, the longer it takes and the more it will cost.

In terms of personal goal setting and having a dream for our lives, we can literally set any grandiose goal we choose, and sometimes we do, especially when we're young. Sometimes however, we set the goal based only on what we think we can achieve. And quite often we get there. And as we get older we may even lower the bar further – making the easy choices. This happens because when we set a goal or a vision for ourselves that seems too lofty or hard to achieve, our internal process orientation side kicks in and we get frustrated because we can't seem to find the resources or best way to get there or we think the price, be it effort, training, time etc. is too high. So we don't go there. We tell ourselves we can't get there and we reset our dream to accommodate our situation. And theses situations can often become cyclical. This means that every time we try to move on or move up we rethink it and end up not moving at all.

But what if we did not settle for only what we knew we could do, and dreamt of something that we really wanted to do? How would our world look then? How do we shift?

Here are a couple of thoughts: As we set our goal, imagine not only reaching it, but also what we would do next. This will help push the dream a bit farther out.

Concentrate on the how the outcome will feel. When considering our vision, we can't focus on what it will take to achieve it, but rather the feeling we get once we arrive.

And finally, even though we may not know how the journey will unfold, we have to maintain the vision and at the very least make a move in the direction by taking some type of action. Whatever our dream may be, there is at least one step we can take, one move we can make toward the dream and once we do, it draws the dream closer. The one step process removes the burden of having to connect all of the dots before we start. With one simple move in the right direction, a commitment of faith, we can set in motion energy of purpose that serves to align the dots on our behalf. All we have to do is believe, point and go.

Szenippet: It serves no purpose to dream and then not make some move to live the dream.

■ ■ ■

Straight On Till Morning
From the Szenabling file:

"Second star to the right and straight on till morning" is one of my favorite lines and it comes from the JM Barrie work Peter Pan. It's a call to a grander greater life - A life of abundance, adventure and joy, a journey to the unknown. An option that is always within reach no matter how stuck or stalled we may feel we have become.

We're taught that control is a variable in happiness. And so it is. When we have freedom and choices and can control our own actions, we have the potential to soar past that second star and beyond. Sometimes though, we view control as its own goal and final destination, and we gain comfort in controlling our surroundings, security, income, children, job etc. We are comforted by the fact that we have eliminated chance from the equation. Events and life itself cease to be unknown. Everything is predictable and known in advance. For some, the end of the day is predetermined before the sun has even cast its first wink of light.

I am not one of those people, not because I don't see the benefit of consistency or predictability, but rather because I have difficulty in following the recipe for how life is supposed to unfold. When morning casts its first shadow for me it brings a hope for what's next and new, not what's today's schedule. It unlocks the unknown, not a rerun. Yes, I do have a generally good idea for what to expect, but for the past few decades, I've been surprised repeatedly. And the reason that happens is pretty simple: I seek the unknown, and I'm open to the possibilities.

Generally speaking though, we all learn to stay the course by seeing what we want and disregarding the rest. By following our plan, we reach objectives and use repetition to insure that the path is clear and consistent. It's a pretty good way to live, and I'm always amazed at the discipline people can bring to bear on their dreams.

I tell you this because I'm happy and proud to be celebrating my son Adam's graduation from college. His very first agenda item was to secure his place at my place, which I'm actually very excited about. As part of the celebration we're heading to New York City for a few days during the first week in June. He's never been, so we'll be doing the tourist thing. If any of you reading this live in New York please let me know. I'd be happy to see you, maybe sign a Book of Szen, or buy you a coffee.

This trip all happened very last minute as I have some business there anyway, but to my point of new horizons and taking that second star to the right, I'd like to introduce Adam to the possibilities, one of which is an interview I've already scheduled for him while we're there – Hey a Dad has to have some control.

Straight on till morning!

Szenippet: The shortest distance between you and happiness is the space between an open and a closed door.

■ ■ ■

Sow What

A Sixty-Word SZEN Story:

It was a whole other day than when they started and it seemed like it could go on forever. Two names were pre-selected and yet there was only the single-minded goal for a healthy baby; Boy or girl would be loved just the same. Then, late in the night, nearly dawn, the spank and the cry rang out. Welcome home.

And more...
Accepting the outcome, whatever it may turn out to be, is a sign of confidence and faith that we can handle and embrace what life sends us. What makes it easy is understanding and recognizing that life usually sends us what we ask for. Like the story above, our actions and thoughts will net out a desired outcome. We get to choose how excited and accepting we will be when our dreams turn into reality.

What we think we want, we draw toward us. Usually, however, there is a gestation period where all of our wishes and hopes morph into actions and plans driven by the simple assumption that we will receive what we seek. We actually create the end result, and the wonder of it all is that whatever it is we want begins with a simple idea, a thought that becomes the seed for what's next.

What might be next for us is up to us. What steps we take are ours alone. What future we enter tomorrow is based on the story we write today. There is a pattern to life, as we know it. Like a baby enters the world, our aspirations and dreams come alive. And to prove it, just look in the rear view mirror to see what we've created so far. Yep, we really do reap what we sow.

Szenippet: We should never doubt our ability to change what is or create something brand new. By simply thinking about what we truly want, our story begins to be rewritten and our dream becomes the reality.

■ ■ ■

CHAPTER 6

When Knowledge is Power

Insights and Ideas That Set Us Free

EDITOR'S NOTES CHAPTER SIX

Calmfidence

Brainality

Point of Contact (we have an impact on everything in our lives)

Changing is Believing

Neutral Zone (don't stay here, it puts your life on stall)

Brain Check (when making choices, doing just consult your brain, also check your feelings.)

Change of Seen** (everyone sees the world differently, explore other people's perspective

Line of Cite (we create stories about experiences to keep our ego intact.)

Blind Spot (watch out for your blind spots.)

Extend the Trend (it feels wonderful when we do our best and complete things)

Watch Your Step (keep nimble with missteps)

Time Consuming (don't consume time, harvest it, repeat)

Calmfidence
SZEN other words:

The biggest difference between then and now in regards to knowledge can be summed up in the affirmation that "learning is not the same as simply having access to information." The world today is literally at our fingertips and virtually anything we want to know we can find out. A fact, figure, trend, and event - you name it - and the Internet will deliver. We have learned how to access the treasure trove of humankind, but how much do we really understand and own?

If knowledge is power, then theoretically we're all equal, in as much as we can all access and absorb the same information. Information has been running rampant for some time, and as it expands to even greater and faster download times we've had to adjust our thinking. The adjustment has been subtle, but noteworthy. We have evolved from learning, studying and understanding things to having the ability to retrieve the relevant information about any thing. It's faster, cleaner and incredible in terms of enabling all of us an equal opportunity at achieving true wisdom.

However, being plugged into just about anything puts pressure on each of us to filter through the random and inexhaustible flood of data, commentary and misperceptions to the real meaningful stuff. What used to take years of reading, studying and analyzing is now already provided. We each have to judge, catalog, discern and package the info into our own unique point of view; sometimes without having done the homework i.e. connecting the dots, identifying the rationale' and ultimately applying what we've learned into a solid, no fooling nougat of knowledge. As we get better at forming our own perspectives, we begin the filtering process and start to turn certain valves of information off and to open others all the way. We begin the process of formalizing principles that we elect to not only live by, but to share. Principles reside at the core of all our beliefs about the world and our relationship to it.

Once we achieve a sense of groundedness in our viewpoint we graduate from mere confidence to calmfidence. No longer do we feel the need to "sell" what we think and know, we can simply put it out there calmly and let it take hold. Calmfidence is the difference between someone that knows that they can call upon information in a nanosecond, and someone that already has assimilated the information they need. In other words, the info is in "context" to life's current situation. Because it's already been filtered and scrutinized it's now ready to use. And this is the key: Information that is unfiltered and unprocessed without a mechanism for pasteurization can be daunting and make us feel out of control.

The beauty of today's fast moving, immediate, interactive and content-rich society is that we have choices and options about what we let into our lives and what we leave out. And all of us have an inner voice that lets us know when we're doing the right thing based on something deeper than a search engine's algorithm. We can feel it, we know it, and a calmness coupled with confidence percolates to the surface. Szen other words – calmfidence.

Szenippet: You can't just believe what your brain tells you; your heart needs to be heard too.

■ ■ ■

Brainality

SZEN other words:

There is an interesting book* that explains how our own brains can short-circuit our path to happiness. It's sitting on the coffee table as I write this. I'm only about eight chapters into it, and I've already had an epiphany. I realize that when I read or am exposed to valuable ideas and concepts, no matter how complicated and detailed the information might be, I try and simplify the input in my own mind so that I can use, remember and even share it. There are so many great thinkers and ideas and theories swirling around us from throughout time, that I've determined that very few of us are going to be able to inhale such a mother lode of good stuff. That said, I'd like to share the "Szen other words" version of some of the good stuff that comes my way.

The brain as we all know is pretty darn powerful. It often can react and perform even if we're not ready for it. It has the power of knowing what things make us happy or afraid, and it tries to provide them to us even if we're not consciously asking for something. The book I'm reading explains that our brain will hot wire thoughts we have over time to the point that they fire on their own. The authors make the point that these messages can be deceptive because they were formed through years of repetition and as a result, really don't care much about what's going on in the present. It's the reason we sometimes revert to old habits because they are so ingrained that we don't even "think" about them anymore. The brain doesn't ask if we want to have a thought or not, it just sends what it's been taught to send.

The good news is that an old brain really can be taught new tricks. Even chronic behavior and addictions can be rewired to the point that our mind is in control again. The mind is the real captain of our voyage through life. It sets the course and sees the distant shores we call goals. The brain is merely the helmsman and steers where we have told it to go. Often we're travelling through time and space without challenging what our brain tells us to do. It's not the brain's fault, it's only trying to make us happy by sending messages we are used to receiving – messages ingrained from childhood that say we're smart or stupid, talented or not, and loved or rejected. The book though makes an excellent point – "you can't always believe what your brain tells you." What this essentially means is that we all have the power to change.

I really like the way this book puts the power back where it belongs. The author quotes numerous studies, medical evidence and real people that have proven that we are not our brains. And if we receive random, disconcerting thoughts that make us feel weird or bad, we don't have to own them, but rather we can blame our brain for sending us old, wrong thoughts based on our past tendencies and actions that really don't reflect where we want to go today. That was then, this is now. It's the brain that remembers what we taught it and it's the brain messages inside that wear us down and make us do things we no longer want to do. The problem is that you can't amputate your brain; you have to retrain it like some mischievous pet that buries your slippers in the back yard.

To that end it's important to remember what's real and what's important. An old, repetitive, deceptive message from your brain that's keeping you from your destiny isn't reality, it's brainality. It's made up, just a signal that we've been pro-grammed to receive and often relish or fear, but it's only just a signal and not real unless or until we accept it as real. If we truly want to navigate to a better place we don't have to find a new helmsman, we just have to find a more accurate and less deceptive (or traumatized) compass.

Szenippet: Reality is often better than many of the things your brain comes up with or wants you to think.

* Inspiration compliments of **You Are Not Your Brain** by Jeffrey M. Schwartz M.D. and Rebecca Gladding M.D. © 2011 All rights reserved.

■ ■ ■

Point of Contact

I subscribe to a belief that nothing is in isolation. Everything and everybody is connected somehow and that every, or even any, action causes a ripple in events and circumstances that generates the potential for lasting change. Sometimes even the most casual gesture like a smile can transform a person's entire day. A frown works the same way. There have been many books on this concept.

Armed with this simple truth of being able to make an impact on literally everyone we meet, it seems that more peo-ple would be reacting more often to whatever signal we're sending and they would consequently be sending us a return signal. After all, we all share the same software, but for some reason, not all that many "connections" really take hold. Is it that we're happy with the connections we already have, or are we trying to avoid the burden of letting someone new into our space? I don't know.

Sometimes we choose to have our antenna down and imagine that we are neither sending nor receiving. But in reality being in the off mode **is** sending a signal. And it's just as true that when we're in the "on" mode ourselves, we recognize the "off" mode in others and back off, (unless we're in sales)

The point is that the opportunities to make contact, to have impact, to change dispositions and to make real and meaningful connections are available to all of us, all the time. All we need is the smile on our face to start and we can join in any time we choose, like now. :)

Szenippet: No touch goes unfelt.

Szenippet: Things will go wrong, but how we handle them gets us right.

■ ■ ■

Changing is Believing
From the Szenabling file:

Years ago I worked with a company that bought another company that was having problems The new owners had big plans to rename, rebrand and re-launch it with very high expectations for success. They kept the previous ownership/management team on to make sure the transition would be painless and efficient. After a few short months, the newly named and re-launched brand was floundering. This left the new owners upset and the previous owners with a sense of vindication.

When we have a choice to change something we might be inclined to keep what works and change what doesn't. It makes a lot of sense, but it's often not that easy to do. That's because we assume that the situation or person we want to change really can be changed. From our perspective, a tweak here or there (a re-brand or a new name) is all that is needed to get back on track. Well that may be true dealing with technology, or patents or brick and mortar locations, but it's almost never true when we're trying to change other people.

Here are three axioms that might be useful to remember if we're trying to create some change in a person or ourselves:

- We cannot change anyone that doesn't want to change. They alone have the power.
- No one can change us if we don't want to. Same reason.
- Change is a process that begins with a goal and a reason to get there. Only when we believe that changing is truly needed, and worth it will we try.

Lessening some pain or creating some gain will move us to act. And in the act of trying we enter the world of compromise and collaboration where anything is possible and goals are achieved. And if we don't try, we'll never know.

Szenippet: By understanding what we want and why we want it, we take the first step on the journey of creation.

■ ■ ■

Neutral Zone

Imagine a neutral zone place where one could go and be safe from all the worries and tribulations of the world, as well as our own personal bugaboos. Imagine that in this place, being non-decisive is okay and avoidance is applauded. In this place, it seems like time has stopped, and it only begins again when we choose to leave.

In the neutral zone, it may appear that we can relax and take our time, but it's a trick. Time really doesn't stop, and it can leave us behind. That's because we're not meant to be neutral, we're designed to keep moving. When we're moving we engage in life, and we can tap into the free adrenaline and energy it provides. Even mistakes and moving the wrong way can provide energy, because failure is only a temporary outcome not a destination.

Wherever we are now, be it building on success or overcoming failure, it's no time to enter the neutral zone, it's no time to stop. It's time to keep moving, to make the most of your time.

Szenippet: If you're stuck on the fence and can't decide, it's better to leap than to fall.

■ ■ ■

Brain Check
From the Now & Szen file:

Over thinking something can create analysis paralysis. It usually happens because we're unsure of some of the facts or afraid of the repercussions of making a mistake. Either way, it can be a painful and sometimes never ending process. There is often no clear logical resolution for some of life's most difficult questions. Yet we seem intent on trying to come up with the answers anyway.

If you find yourself with an especially tricky or perplexing decision, it sometimes helps to turn off the brain and relax a bit. The brain will strive to be absolute and sometimes it's just not possible to know for sure, exactly what to do. The choices then become:

Do nothing, and whatever happens, happens.
Take your best shot and hope it works out.
Just go with what "feels" right and live with the outcome.

The latter has the best chance usually because it includes the important component of "living with the outcome." When we're prepared to live with the results of our decisions, we gain control of the situation in as much as we're at least moving toward a conclusion. In the movement alone toward a desired effect, we gain positive momentum because a step made with faith pays dividends no matter what happens.

Following what "feels" right is often hard to explain, but it can calm our heart knowing we're following its lead. The *inner voice*, the *heart's calling*, *following your gut* -whatever you want to call it is a very real and valuable sextant for guiding our decisions. And decisions made on our feelings are ultimately what define us and make us unique. Our brains may be able to agree on facts and data, but only our hearts know what's really right for us.

Check your brain and let the feelings reign – Feeling better already.

Today's Szenippet: Less judging, more peace.

■ ■ ■

Change of Seen

From the Szenabling file:

I had a conversation with a friend and we were discussing a dinner we had together some time ago. I remember the dinner being exceptionally well prepared and loving the ambience of the restaurant, the excellent service and the engaging conversation - All in all a delightful and memorable night in my mind. My friend's recollection of the evening was cloudy at best if not contrary to my view. She had forgotten what the conversation was about, and the name of the restaurant, but thought the food was average or below.

I started wondering if we were discussing the same night. How can two people experience the exact same thing and yet be so far apart in their interpretation? The short answer is that it happens all of the time to everybody. We all have distractions, pre-conceived notions, beliefs and other filters that we engage to create our very own version of reality. What happens then, if we don't explore others' perspective on events and other matters, is that we assume our view is the correct and only view. This is called the Tetris effect: we see what we look for and miss the rest.

In an experiment as told in *The Happiness Advantage*, volunteers watch a video of two basketball teams – one wearing white shirts and the other wearing black ones – who are passing around a basketball. The viewers have to count the number of times the white team passes the ball. About 25 seconds into the video a person in a full gorilla costume walks straight through the action traveling across the screen for a full 5 seconds. Afterwards viewers were asked if they had noticed anything unusual in the video., did you notice the giant gorilla? Amazingly, nearly half (46%) missed the gorilla and actually refused to believe it until they were shown the video again, and of course there it was, as big as life.

What's interesting is that we don't always have a way to see the video again nor would we even be inclined to want to check. And so, imagine how much we may miss or get completely wrong about things that happen in our life every single day. And imagine how many people may misinterpret our actions or words and are left with a completely erroneous understanding of what we intended. And worse, when there are no words or actions at all, we will assume whatever we want. That assumption then becomes what we truly believe. And with no follow up questions from a researcher to test our beliefs, we base new decisions and insights on wobbly if not completely wrong thinking, often leaving a trail of missed opportunities.

Every once in a while though, we can have a *change of seen* where we are able to see a past event in a new reality

- information that was missed is suddenly found or new facts emerge. When we are open to new information or possibilities, we begin to see an expanded reality that is less filtered, a reality, which could possibly change our future by simply reexamining our past. If there is something you're not quite sure of or have lingering doubts about, what really happened, take another look. You may be surprised to see a gorilla.

Today's Szenippet: The way we see the world is the only way that matters.

■ ■ ■

Line of Cite
From the Now & Szen file:

Our mind is a battlefield of thoughts, each fighting for enough attention and energy to be acted upon. In the world of thought wrestling, I've come to the conclusion that there are forces at play that impact which thought survives and ultimately gets created.

In the school of thought arena, I like to believe that everything happens for a reason, which I call a "connect the dots" way of thinking. The opposite of connect the dots is *randomness rules*; whatever happens, happens. These two very different worlds when they clash create a lot of brain residue, because typically our minds seek order not chaos. But when things just happen for no apparent reason, we can sometimes get dislodged from our default focal point of strength and find ourselves in a high-speed reaction mode. In other words, when something happens that we're just not prepared for, we have to think fast; not just about our reactions, but also about the explanation of why it happened at all.

Regardless the actual event, we tend to develop the appropriate story to explain the situation, even though we seemingly may have had nothing to do with its occurrence. Sometimes we'll refer to evidence we can cite that supports the event. Or sometimes we'll shrug and suggest a notion like "accidents do happen." As long as the event is justified or rationalized somehow, we're able to move on. And why is this so critical? It matters because without some closure we can't move forward.

Like a writer that maintains a character's integrity throughout the story, we often will create the story after the fact to maintain our own integrity. So even if it was a random event, we'll develop a *connect the dots* scenario to explain it. This ability underscores our complicated nature and need for something definitive to ground us. The explanation becomes the crutch and tool we need to grow. It helps explain why things like relationships or jobs didn't work out, why our children did not make the team and why letting the bet ride, seemed like a good idea at the time.

In essence, we can think anything we want to, to serve any purpose we choose, and be perfectly comfortable with the outcome. We have that kind of power. We possess the ability to create events or, at the very least, stories about events, that will fit our life's movie. With a clear line of cite, where explanations, real or fabricated, are identified and sourced, we can advance and so can the audience of our life advance with us.

Connecting the loose dots helps us survive. It helps put things into perspective and context for sharing, which we need to do in order to let go and move on. It's the sharing, that outside endorsement that we seek. When we share our view of whatever happened, we're simply asking for acceptance, or sympathy or something that makes it okay so we can process it and make room for what's next. And it's the *what's next*, foreseen or not, that helps our story unfold and keeps it interesting.

Today's Szenippet: Even a bad story makes sense to the person telling it, whereas a good story makes sense to everybody.

What makes a true story great is the dash of fiction thrown in by the storyteller.

■ ■ ■

Blind Spot

A Sixty-Word SZEN Story:

His thoughts were swirling and bouncing off the walls of his new reality. How in the world did it get to this - a yes or no phone call? He had been unassailable and lived his life accordingly, without fear, but not now. What happens next changes everything. He stood, took a long breath and picked up the phone: "hello?"

And more...

Reality has a way of sneaking up on us. Often when we're surprised by some new fact or discovery, we wonder why it took so long to recognize it. We sometimes develop blind spots to information that does not conform to our thinking. We live too long with first impressions and misunderstandings. We choose to close our eyes to what everyone else seems to see but us.

A case in point occurred to me last weekend while on a trip to Chicago. I was at a post wedding party in the backyard, loving the sunny weather and the company. I had placed my sunglasses on the table for a few minutes and when I went to retrieve them, something was different. They were the same designer label and model and fit as perfectly as ever. They were however a different color. They were black and my glasses were brown. No problem I thought, it's a common brand and someone had mistakenly made the switch. I asked around, explaining what happened, but no luck.

I started to play back in my mind who the culprit might have been and suggested they look around a little closer. Then I became resolved that whoever it was had left the party unaware and would discover their mistake and, like me, get a chuckle from the mix-up. But no one came forward. So as I repeated the story with a sense of wonder and humor or the next couple of days, I realized that I had become a bit obsessed with the mystery and was even able to recruit others on my quest.

Eventually though I shifted and actually preferred the black. I began to see it as a lucky exchange of fate. I wondered if my sons who gave me the glasses for my birthday would notice the difference. After parading with the glasses on before their eyes, I was astonished that they didn't pick up on the obvious color change. I finally asked if they noticed any difference and the answer was a resounding "no!" As I explained what happened, fully expecting to convince them, they said: "Dad, they've always been black, you're such a goof. You're color blind."

I guess it's official. I have not only lost my mind, but my ability to trust my judgment, at least when it comes to color. My apologies to those that suffered through my story and interrogations; I plead temporary insanity caused by a chronic blind spot that let me see only what I believed, but not the truth.

Szenippet: Erasing the blind spots in our inner vision lets us truly see not only what is, but also what could be.

■ ■ ■

Extend The Trend
A Sixty-Word SZEN Story:

Liz knew how to play the game. She understood that for everything she obtained there was a price. She reached the perfect balance of ins and outs, ups and downs, and over and unders to begin to feel at ease. It just felt right to be in charge. From here there would be no stopping her. She had finally arrived.

And more...
When we do what it takes to navigate our lives through the challenges and turmoil that life sends, it feels good to reflect for a moment and pat ourselves on the back for a job well done. Success, closure, and some semblance of a comfort zone are all signs that we have placed ourselves in a space and time that feels good and safe. In effect we have taken charge of our condition and current situation in order to provide a shelter and respite to be able to enjoy the moment.

Accomplishments, and simply finishing something that we need to tackle provides a sense of completion and often pride. Even activities like shoveling snow, cleaning the house or making a great dinner can provide a sense of joy for the mere fact that it's done, over and complete and more importantly it was done well.

We know when we give our best, and we know how much better it feels when we do. We also know that whenever we reach a personal best in anything, it opens the door for something even better the next time. We all have the potential to go beyond "arriving" and traverse our way to even greater achievements, and just like Liz in our story we can *extend the trend*. Seeking more and expecting more from ourselves allows us to build and to grow and as long as we view each success as a no parking zone and not the ultimate end, we'll always be able to become better versions of ourselves; a worthy goal worth repeating.

Szenippet: When we find ourselves in a perfect situation, it's not time to stop; it's time to refuel for the next perfect situation.

■ ■ ■

Watch Your Step

Once when I was coming down the stairs where I live and close to the bottom of the outside stairwell, a stair collapsed beneath me and I slipped and fell forward a couple of steps to the cement at the bottom of the stairs. I had my hands full of trash and yet managed to land on my feet with a bit of a thud without dropping an eggshell.

I turned to see what happened behind me and the wooden step had cracked and broken clean away from the steel studs that held it in place. I felt very fortunate that I had "fast reflexes and that I didn't crash and burn. It got me to thinking though that as a metaphor for life that the steps that we plan on taking to our goal can be weak or wobbly, unclear, hidden or just non-existent. When we hit something on our path to our own greatness that knocks us off course, it can be frustrating and sometimes devastating.

If you've ever been forced to create a new route or retrace your steps it can get you thinking about your pace and even the weight you carry on our journey. If a step is lost on a ladder or across a chasm it may not be an option to return and start over. When that happens, count your blessings and keep going. We weren't meant to retreat anyway.

Wherever you may be on our journey and however difficult or easy as the steps may be now, know that you may encounter some loose footing from time to time, but how you handle these missteps – going around, stopping, or even leaping and stumbling ahead will help define the journey and make the next steps you take that much more pivotal.

Szenippet: No path is permanent. Things change and how we navigate and set a new course is what ultimately defines us.

■ ■ ■

Time Consuming
A Sixty-Word SZEN Story:

Ben, the company's newest hire, stood by the water cooler watching the faces of the people file by, answering the bell to return to their stations. What a moment before had been a lunchroom filled with laughter, now turned somber and some-how slower. He had been interrupted mid sentence, silenced by the signal to stop having fun – time to work.

And more...
It's widely considered to be true that "time flies when we're having fun." The opposite holds true as well in that time seems to stop when we're not engaged with the task at hand. Whether it's a boring class, predictable work or a family get together, time will seem to slow to a crawl when we'd rather be someplace else. So the question is that if time slows in these situations, do we actually live longer? Can we actually watch and wait for a pot to boil and never age? Maybe, but who would want to try?

We're not wired to sustain, we're programmed to thrive and if we can be in the places, or with the people and thoughts that engage and enliven us, we'll come to view those moments as precious and in the now; no past, no future, no time. Yes the clock might leap ahead as a reminder that we missed watching it for a while, but we'll have spent, or perhaps *invested* is a better term, in being in a state of now, a place where good things can happen and time can both stop and yet be flying as fast as the fun.

It's comes down to a simple matter of perspective. When we are doing what we want and like, we cease consuming time and begin to harvest it. We glean the best a moment can offer and then move on to the next, and the next and the next, thus creating a string of mindful attachment that can weave a tapestry of joy - where the passage of time becomes an after thought to our experience and not the focus. A place where in our lives, there's no time to watch the clock and really no need.

Szenippet: With every tick and tock a moment presents itself for living, and if not noticed, it will leave.

CHAPTER 7

Taking Chances

Life's Risks worth Risking for Great Rewards

What's the Difference?

Win, Lose or Draw (make decisions from a position of strength, leave your comfort zone)

Un-Fickle Finger (open the door to fate, don't be afraid of your future)

Pretend Acting (act like you are successful and you will be. Reap what you Sow Analogy)

Inside Connections (take responsibility for your current state, go inside and figure out your future)

Got Male (love trumps fear, be with those you love)

Rate My Professor (when we are doing something we love, it shows in our energy and our attitude)

No Last Chances (even if the outcome doesn't go your way, there are always new chances)

On the Fence (jump in and make choices, don't be afraid.)

The Empathy Engine (turn on your empathy and create closer connections)

The Human Baton (our emotions are contagious. Jazz up your life)

Assumptive Silence (don't make assumptions without Asking, speak up for yourself)

What Difference Do You Make

I know that I've talked about the balance in the universe before. I know that for every yin there is a yang, for an up a down, and for a win a loss. I wonder sometimes, especially when I observe people living so long and in such pain on the down side of life, if that up side will ever appear and change everything.

I pray that there is always a way out of whatever muck and mire we face. There is always a chance at greatness and peace and true love. There is always hope that debilitating patterns can be broken and that new horizons will appear. I pray that whatever fears we face can be erased. I cheer for those that see beyond the pain and embrace the hope for calm – for those that should have lost hope, but never give up. I cheer for the real heroes of life; People like you.

Yes, it's you. You get through, get by, get over and conquer the setbacks that life dishes out. You survive and then you thrive. You overcome and emerge anew. You know that there is always a way to win, and that belief and mantra somehow makes a difference - A difference for you and for those that you love and those that love you.

You have the power to make whatever situation you're in better, and when you choose to use it, it's awesome. It could be a smile, a nod, an embrace or a life-changing word. It's all in you and waiting for the right time and place to change a world. You can and will make a difference. You must make a difference; it's why you're here.

Szenippet: When we encounter a death in our lives, there forever lingers the memory of the life that came before it expired, as well as the joy of retelling the story of that life again and again – no one ever dies that owns a place in our hearts.

■ ■ ■

Win, Lose or Draw
From the Szenabling file:

So many decisions we make, especially important ones, work out best when we approach them from a position of strength. Being in charge, acting on desire instead of just need, while controlling the variables gives us the power to call the shots in our favor. These are the times we relish because we know we can't lose; it's only a matter of how much we'll win. It's like having really good choices for deciding what job offer or scholarship to take.

One the other hand, many significant decisions emerge from weakness and happen because we really don't feel we have a choice. And in those situations, we just end up compromising and taking the least worrisome route or often whatever is left to take. It's not about winning at all; it's about not losing too much. Like staying in a bad job just for the health benefits.

A draw is a situation that can keep us even. Not too many highs and not too many lows, somewhere in the nether world of neutral. Whereas a winner's mentality is to keep going, like getting a push hand at the blackjack table usually means they'll try another hand. Winners figure if they bet it once and didn't lose, they might as well try it again and maybe win. The same hand for a losing mentality nets the same re-deal, but with the anticipation for a loss. Both tend to get what they're looking for eventually.

There are also lots of things that turn out to be *draws* in life but with seemingly no option to re-deal. Some situations we negotiated, or compromised ourselves into, are just going to be, by their very nature, somewhere in the middle between winning and losing. These situations are neither painful nor blissful. They just are.

Over time, what happens when the cards we're dealt are just too predictable, and we find ourselves in an endless draw state of mind, is we take the chance of getting bored with the game or worse yet, we fall asleep at the wheel, just going through the motions. Without any highs or lows, we end up in the middle - A perpetual comfort zone that many would say "that's a good thing." Some wouldn't.

If we find ourselves wondering about leaving the comfort zone we created, and we think we might want to shake it up or reshuffle our deck, the first thing to remember is that it's a new game and a win/lose option is a real possibility. Well, do you feel lucky?

Szenippet: Taking something or someone for granted sets the course for loss.

■ ■ ■

Un-fickle Finger
From the Szenabling file:

We all have a comfort zone that we've carefully crafted to suit our lives just fine, thank you. Everything from the time we wake, the coffee we make, and the route to work or school we take, plus a lot of the stuff in between. We tend to like things to be a certain way – our way. And so when opportunity knocks, it is evaluated by the impact it will have on our comfort zone. Not coincidently, some of the best opportunities would easily rip our comfort zones to shreds. That's because *opportunity* and its sister *change* often arrive in the same package. *Change* is often dressed like a price tag.

There is a price to opportunity only because it needs fertile ground to plant its seed and really isn't able to wedge itself into our lives. Opportunity requires that we embrace it and not resist. When opportunity knocks, it expects us to walk through the door and not simply peek through the keyhole. And contrary to popular belief, opportunity doesn't always just knock once; it often will hold its un-fickle finger on the doorbell until we answer. That's because it's custom made for each of us. And if we thought about it, we'd remember that it is exactly what we ordered for ourselves during that time when we still believed in dreams. But somehow we forgot why we wanted it or just gave up waiting for it.

When something we were expecting or wanting isn't delivered in a timely way, , we adapt and learn to do without. There's a good chance we created a "work around" and got good and comfortable without it. But guess what? Dreams still can come true. We just have to believe and leave the comfort zone for a peek at what could be the most exciting, albeit uncomfortable, journey into a better life and future. Open the door. Whatever opportunity we seek might still be there waiting or maybe something better has taken its place; you won't know unless you swing it wide open and say hello.

Szenippet: Be ready to change your life when the un-fickled finger of fate points your way. Fate, it turns out is not random; it's customized to your dreams.

■ ■ ■

Pretend Acting
From the Szenabling file:

With a new year comes new thinking and a new set of resolutions, and sometimes a brand new vision. A vision does not begin with a just dream or some lofty aspiration. It begins simply enough with a decision and then another and another etc. – a combination of thinking and taking action.

> You should take a few moments to make sure that what you ultimately sow is what you ultimately want to reap, because you are now reaping whatever you've been sowing for years. Yes, I'm afraid it's true. We are the products of our own decision making and choosing. The cumulative effect was formed by an incredibly and masterfully formulated series of encounters over time that offered us a chance to make decisions on how things would evolve. The results of all of those decisions are what have brought us to this exact moment

in time — a moment like so many previous and unnoticed moments in the past, which unfortunately, failed
at the time to inspire us to change the nature of our
future.
From the Book of Szen

To change our future this time and to make the process a little
easier as we move to the new better version of ourselves, we
can practice pretend acting. This means we start to pretend
and act as if what we want to accomplish has already occurred.
If we can begin to see the present from our future thinking
minds-eye we will begin to make decisions that align us to
that which we seek. This results in actually changing our belief
about ourselves and helps negate any possible self-sabotage.
The more faith the better the outcomes and the more trust
we have that we are moving in the right direction and making
choices that help us truly reap our dreams.

Szenippet: Whenever we make a choice, we create an outcome. Make good choices and thrive.

■ ■ ■

Inside Connections
From the Szenabling file:

Self-reflection often leads to self-revelation. And the reason
this happens is that we carry our total history with us and have
easy access to memories (not always the short-term ones) and
events that have helped shape us into us. These memories
often carry clues to our thinking at the time that we actually

created the memory. In other words by contemplating the thoughts we were having before something happened, we can determine if those thoughts actually created the event.

By examining our own inside connections and studying the cause and effect nature of what we create for ourselves, we gain insights into how we approach life and what our true beliefs are. This is a valuable exercise, especially when we are experiencing a change in our lives, because it enables us to actually predict what will happen next. That's right! It's a truism that we will reap what we sow and those seeds are created by our own thoughts. Plant something positive, we win. Plant something negative and sure enough, we lose.

Sometimes however, we forget to plant at all and we stop thinking about what we may want, and get stuck thinking about what we already have. This creates a repetitive loop that guarantees the same results and reality over and over. As a student, teacher and advocate for positive change I can testify that nothing new will come into our lives until we break the cycle. And once broken, the seeds for change can take root and bring us into our new reality – a reality created from the inside out.

If we explore the feelings we've had in our happiest moments, we'll discover that we (our thoughts) created those moments. So doesn't it stand to reason that we can duplicate the process and change our lives to whatever we desire? Of course we can. Here are a couple of ideas:

- Wishful thinking and blind faith serves no purpose. In order to attain that which we seek we must believe that we deserve it and then move toward it and take some action to make it happen.

- We must use our own internal compass to set the course. Only we can know our heart's true desire. If we feel we're on our right path, we'll have confidence to pick up the pace and (I'm not sure how this works, but it does) then what we seek will actually move toward us in kind.
- Any seed we plant, regardless of its size, needs to be nurtured in order to bloom. We must mind the soil of our dreams to keep the weeds of doubt away.

Remember that all of the great people in our lives and the laughter and joy that they have brought and continue to bring are with us here and now because some time ago, we thought that's what we wanted.

And, on a personal note, I've been thinking of you for quite a while. Thanks for being in my life.

Szenippet: The key to the future is found when we take responsibility for how we arrived to the here and now.

■ ■ ■

You've Got Male
From the Szenabling file:

Over the past few months as some of you know, I've been involved in the world of on-line dating. It's a world of rejection, fear and hope. It's 24/7 and although the names and the faces change constantly, the profiles and the messaging is eerily consistent. After a while I run out of energy and retreat. Ironically, when this happens, my productivity in the other aspects of my life tends to increase, and I embrace my challenges and opportunities with more vigor and enthusiasm. This makes me feel better and more connected to clients and students and friends. It's exactly the time when I'm at my very best version of Gary.

When I'm in this state I start to absorb everything around me in a "connect the dots" kind of way. I uncover new insights and appreciation for just how beautiful and elegant life can be. I gobble up books and extract new nougats of knowledge to add layers of new thought onto the solid foundation of positive thinking and loving that has always served me well. It draws me into self-evaluation and revelation and I simply gush with a revitalized sense of purpose and wonder. There is just so much to share and inspire that it spills uncontrollably out of me to anyone within earshot. Some of you reading this know exactly what I mean. It's also when I miss love's open arms the most.

That's because love, in my view, presents a safe haven and allows us to strip away fear and gain access to our untethered soul that is our endless potential. Love added to the mix can ignite the possibilities way beyond what a single person can do. And so the search continues for just the right soul mate that can also see their own unlimited potential and appreciate how a simple joining of forces can change the world.

Szenippet: Love trumps fear and without fear we thrive.

■ ■ ■

Rate My Professor

From the Now & Szen file:

In preparation of teaching another school term this summer, I spent some time reviewing the available resources and curriculum for my upcoming course on Branding. I've been teaching this same course for a number of years, and although it's always new and current in terms of discussion and case studies, some of the material is repeated over and over. One such piece is a video that the school made a couple of years ago that shows me in the classroom (it was empty for the filming) basically presenting some of the key tools we use during the course.

It can be painful to watch oneself and I noticed right away that I seemed "flat" and a bit detached. Without any students, I was very self-conscious and aware of the camera, and so it just all seemed a bit stiff and honestly too painful to watch. So I fast-forwarded it a few minutes. When I resumed I immediately saw a new me. I was transformed - same clothes and setting, but a new vibrant, energized and all together engaging guy.

What happened is that once I became comfortable with the setting, I was able to simply share what I knew. And because I so love what I do, the enthusiasm and energy became obvious. I think I actually looked a lot younger and certainly more involved and animated. This all reminded me of a couple of things, some concepts, that we all know and yet can easily forget. The first is that we absolutely project whatever it is we're feeling inside. Pain, discomfort, fear...whatever it is that's going on...ends up on the screen for everyone to see.

The second idea is that when we are doing something we love, it brings us to life. If we just look around at everyone we see or meet, we can tell when they are living in their sweet spot and truly enjoying life. We can see it in their faces and smiles and also how the people they are interacting respond–it's as if they are in a zone. There is something authentic about them that everyone sees. That's why salespeople that believe in their product make the most sales. It's how an impassioned minister draws a larger congregation. And it's why we can't stop ourselves from buying Girl Scout cookies.

We all have something that brings us to life. And when the switch gets flipped on, we begin to glow. So the goal then is to turn in on as often as we can and keep it on as long as we can. In other words, when we find something that makes us happy we should simply do more of it. It makes sense I think, that we would all be more fun to be around if the switch was always on. So that's this week's homework. Find what makes you happy, practice it all week, and report back to me. If you can't find anything, let me know and I'll assign you something. You will be graded. Good luck.

Today's Szenippet: If there is not enough happiness in your life, maybe it's because you closed the intake valve. It's worth a check.

■ ■ ■

No Last Chances

A Sixty-Word SZEN Story:

Robert fumbled for his key, cursing the darkness. She would have to believe that he intended to be there, but everything was going wrong and now in the 11th hour he panicked and prayed. Would she wait? She had said this was his last chance. Just then the key found his hand. He hit the gas..."Hang on Angel, I'm coming..."

And more...
So often we begin with positive and purposeful intentions, but sometimes circumstances don't cooperate. And as much as we truly desire and pray for a particular outcome, obstacles can appear out of nowhere that can stymie us. It then becomes a matter of will and desire. How much do we want what we seek and what price will we pay? In many of our wishes, the "things" we want do have a price tag. We weigh the decision and either write the check or not, knowing that there will be new and different choices later. In matters of the heart however, it's not so simple.

The intangibles of our life like joy and peace and love etc. cannot be bought and sold. They can only be given and received. We can't really own any of it, but we can enjoy the experience and make decisions and take actions that put us in the right spots at the right time to feel the power of affection and appreciation. Sometimes these "spots" can be lifetimes or momentary encounters and they always have the potential to shift. In matters of the heart we may think we've arrived and are okay just where we stand, but when the floor beneath us still moves, we can find the shakiness unnerving as that "sweet spot" of love has retreated, resigned or somehow been removed.

When left behind and alone, we freeze with fear and of loss. We wrongly think that there are no more chances left. We fail to see the cycle of how peace and joy and all of the feelings of living in a state of hope and the now still remain. We might panic and fumble to find the key, but we **will** find it, and we will be right where we intended to be. Like Robert, we're never too late to take a chance and hit the gas to take us exactly where we want to be.

Szenippet: The destination we seek resides in our hearts not on a vision board.

■ ■ ■

On the Fence
A Sixty-Word SZEN Story:

The mailbox was filled with invitations. Each one sounding more appealing. Alice was excited by the possibilities. Which one to accept, whom to go out with? Post divorce, she was enjoying having the opportunity to explore new pathways. But overtures meant decisions and that made her sad, frozen and on the fence.

And more...
Life offers up such great opportunities and possibilities that's it's often difficult to make a choice. And so we ponder, which can lead to analysis and even worry. What if we choose wrong?

What then? What do we do? Well, we could stay on the fence in a limbo state, withdraw to our previous side of the fence, or leap off of the fence into our new decision.

Is there a way to be sure that the job selection, or the bet, or this new person is the absolute, positive, winning, clear and guaranteed correct choice? Nope. Sorry. However, when we're stuck we can still make some moves. Here are a few options:

> Do nothing – Not making a decision puts us at the whim of nature and the will of others. Doing nothing means giving up control and in that scenario all we can do is take what we get.
> Fall back – Retreating to the space and time before the decision was upon us can sometimes be an option. Going in reverse and retreating means we've shrunk back into a known comfort zone and in that world we rationalize that everything is really fine; really.
> Jump in – It might seem like we're taking a chance on a choice when we have no proof, but it's really less of a chance than we think. Leaping into the other side of the fence actually creates positive energy for the decision. In effect, our choice is a type of commitment and therein lies a power to turn the unsure into a "count me in" reality.

All of the above are actually decisions in their own right, but they vary by the level of commitment it will take to really achieve what we desire. The fact that we face choices at all means we're moving and searching and that action reveals opportunities. The thing to remember is that we're causing the choices to emerge and we've attracted our options that require our decision. And the results can only be known only after the decision is actually made.

Don't be afraid Alice, you'll be fine.

Szenippet: A decision is also a commitment to the intended result.

■ ■ ■

The Empathy Engine
A Sixty-Word SZEN Story:

"What in the world were these people doing?" she wondered. First one, then two, then everybody else that was stopped at the light got out of their cars and walked away. Lisa panicked and checked her mirrors and then turned all the way around in her seat to see who was left. Only her, then the light turned green

And more...

Sometimes it's not enough to simply know about a person, often we need to understand what they might be feeling and *why* they feel it to truly make a connection. Being able to put ourselves "in the shoes" of another allows us a clear passage for communication and relationship to begin. That's why empathy is the single most valuable tool we have as humans to create positive change for all those that cross our path and ourselves too.

As simple as the concept of empathy is, to appreciate its power and to use it properly takes not only an open-minded perspective and supportive nature, but also practice and discipline. It doesn't work like the switch of a light that we can turn on and off at will, but rather it is a commitment that must remain in the on position to have the greatest impact.

To understand the implications of empathy on relationship all we need to do is to recall a circumstance where another person has sought to truly understand us and appreciate our situation. Once we believe that someone cares enough to consider what we're feeling, we tend to open the share gates even further and reach back, in kind, to improve the connection. And it's these connections, be it business or personal that propels us to seek our true purpose for being. The residual essence of discovering that purpose is what creates our own personal wake and ultimate legacy.

The place to start creating lasting and meaningful relationships that are aligned with our own personal dharma is to remember that everyone has a unique story that is still unfolding. By practicing empathy, we are able to read another's plot and character development. Thus we can create better and more personalized interactions. Then we can introduce our own story in its proper and most illuminating context. And once the stories merge, the possibilities are endless.

To start our own journey using empathy as our engine we need to get our story straight right now. Where are we really and what will the next chapters reveal? Will circumstance draw us to new people; will we draw others to us? Will we be mindful of what others are doing and what would we do if we found ourselves alone like Lisa and the light turned green?

Whatever story we craft, the ending will be happier once we get to understand and appreciate the rest of the characters and their stories too.

Szenippet: At the core of trust is the assumption that the other person really "gets" me.

■ ■ ■

The Human Baton
A Sixty-Word SZEN Story:

Elaine stopped at the red light and glanced at her rear-view mirror to witness a young woman in the car behind her bouncing in her seat. The arms flailed about and although Elaine couldn't hear anything, it appeared by the way her mouth moved that she was singing. It made her smile. Next light, Elaine burst into song delighting the driver just ahead.

And more...
I think it's amazing how contagious certain actions can become. A smile, frown, and a yawn evoke a sameness in response. All that we do, be it at home, work, or play is observed by others and how we go about what we do sends a signal to all that observe. And these signals don't have to have any verbal cues for a telling message to be sent on how we're feeling.

The ability to understand the relationship between verbal and non-verbal communication is a gift we all possess. We all can tell when our team feels defeated even though they are still shouting encouragement to each other. The body language never lies. And in the same way if someone is asking you to trust them, but can't look you straight in the eye, it's a sign to be wary.

I share all of this because this gift we have is great on the receiving end. But if we use it as a way to send it's even more powerful. Like our friend Elaine, who by simply observing someone, having fun in the moment with a song, was able to apply the "feeling" and keep the chain going.

I suggest we consider the impact we can have by simply changing our demeanor, facial expression and energy level to impart something positive to another. Try it at work, or at home with the kids. Take a routine and "jazz" it up a bit. I'll bet you'll not only get noticed, you'll get connected and possibly be able to pass the human baton of good feelings to someone that could really use it and who will pass it on as well. Let me know how it goes.

Szenippet: What's in our heart always bubbles up to influence the way we act, look and are perceived. There is no denying its power or promise to turn any moment into a new journey.

■ ■ ■

Assumptive Silence
A Sixty-Word SZEN Story:

Roberta heard her name on the news and that the evidence against her was adding up fast. The detective said: "An eyewitness puts this woman at the scene of the crime, and we're just waiting for the warrant." "No one interviewed me," she thought. "They think I did it, but they're just plain wrong." She wondered: "Should I talk?"

And more...
Speaking up for ourselves is something that most of us take for granted. We are happy to say what we think if someone asks a question or needs to know something specific about our work etc. But what if someone prefers NOT to hear our point of view. What if they avoid us or never give us a chance to say what's on our mind? What then? What happens?

Silence, whether we create it by not speaking, or if there is no chance to speak, creates a void that in the absence of real facts and information is filled with assumptions. When people don't ask, it is because they probably don't want to know and prefer to assume the answer. And because assumptions eventually turn into beliefs, anyone can make up whatever scenario they choose. We all can. If we really want to live with what we "think" we know, we can. And the same holds true for people that may consider what we think to be disruptive or counter to their assumptions.

Assumptions are made all of the time because we don't have the time to know everything we need to know. So we guess and fill in the blanks with conjecture and opinion. Saves time and arguments. But sometimes like Roberta, it's important to be heard. And it's our responsibility to find a way to get what needs to be said, said. The bottom line is that assumptions of any kind can trigger actions and reactions that may be unfair, unwise, or as Roberta said, "just plain wrong." Why take a chance? Let what we know come out and seek from others what's inside of them. Reality and the truth therein is a much easier place to start to change our world. And don't assume it can't be done.

Szenippet: People like to have order in their thinking. So if you don't tell them what you think, they will think what they want. They will think that they know what you think - Silence begets assumption.

■ ■ ■

CHAPTER 8

The Szend

Coming to the Szend of the Book

EDITOR'S NOTES FOR CHAPTER EIGHT

THE SZEND OF THE BOOK

Belief

Momentum

What If

A Knew Day

Goal Post

Letting go of Expectations (let go of worry about controlling the outcome of things and free yourself)

Belief

To believe in someone - letting him or her know that we have the trust and faith to support them on whatever journey they choose - is often the only fuel they will ever need to succeed.

Szenippet: Genuine encouragement given freely can ignite the spark of miracles.

■ ■ ■

Momentum

The definition of momentum (*mo* for short) is: The quantity of motion of a moving body, measured as a product of its mass and velocity. However one may define it, it is an advantage to have it. And once lost, it is often difficult to regain. Momentum is often traded in contests where one person or team versus another. It's been said to have a flow and is often the difference in who wins. It's often fickle and we can actually "feel" it come and go, as well as see it in action in others.

If we want momentum on our side and in our lives, here's a tip: We have to take action. Momentum doesn't just come when called; it arrives only if we're moving. By taking steps toward our goals, even if only baby steps, we can gain an impetus and a confidence. The more we act, the more we gain. So set the course and start moving and may the wind of *mo* be at your back.

Szenippet: No step in pursuit of greatness is ever wasted.

■ ■ ■

What If?
A Sixty-Word SZEN Story:

"There is this event coming up soon", she started, "actually it's upon us, and I was wondering if maybe, you would like ummm, well I mean.., if I were to ask you, hypothetically speaking, to go with me to this event, what would you say?" "Yes of course." I replied. "Hey not so fast!" She blurted. "Nobody's asked you yet."

And more...

Wouldn't it be nice to know the answer to every question we ask before we ask it? Isn't it true that we can find ourselves in situations where the answer we seek will not be found and we become afraid of what the real answer will be? Don't we sometimes even pass altogether on asking because we can't bear the possibility of rejection or maybe, like the story above, the possibility of acceptance?

Asking questions is the purest form of being assertive, curious and to some extent fearless. When we confront an issue and rely on another to give us an answer, we take a chance on getting a response we won't like. And we also close the gaps in communication and replace questions with knowledge. If we don't ask, we won't know for sure, and then we'll be left filling in our own answers that become our default beliefs. If we follow this logically for only a few more consecutive questions, based on our own assumptions, we could easily find ourselves in a communications quagmire – a place of misinformation and speculation.

On the other hand if we ask clearly, we will know and maybe even receive. It seems so easy, but it can be tough to do, especially when the other person has some authority or power over us, like a parent or a boss. The key is to remind ourselves that we can always make better decisions when we're dealing with the facts. Knowledge is power and asking directly for what we want or need will actually put us in the driver's seat. In assertiveness training, we learn to ask even the hard questions. The more we take responsibility to ask, the easier it gets and the more we learn. It's simple: If you don't ask, you won't know. "When's that event again?"

Szenippet: "Ask and you shall receive" is always true even if we don't like what we get.

■ ■ ■

A Knew Day
A Sixty-Word SZEN Story:

Ted felt strangely omnipotent as if he were viewing the scene from afar or in a movie. He seemed able to perceive and recognize the inner voices of everyone in the room. Not the words that he heard, but the internal messages and thoughts behind them. For most he perceived a lag time from thought to utterance - All except Marsha.

And more...
Sometimes we can predict what people will say or do, and sometimes we can't. There are times when the radar and antenna are picking up all the signals we need to assimilate in advance of the very sentence that's about to come out of someone's mouth. And sometimes we're clueless and ill prepared for what we're about to hear or see.

The simple explanation is that we perceive better when we put our attention to something. If we're "listening" and open to what might be happening right now around us we can pick up signals and vibrations that create insights or even an advance preview or notice of an encounter. We can actually train ourselves to accurately predict what might next occur. In reality, we do it all of the time already. Any regular or routine activity, after a short time, can become predictable and we are able to move effortlessly, with rote confidence, through work, or chores, or even relationships with a pretty high degree of certainly that everything is as it should be.

If we're not careful, each day can become a "knew" day and we find ourselves going through the motions or like Ted we somehow know what's going to happen before it happens. Where's the fun in that? That's why it's important, like Ted, to have a bit of Marsha in our lives - No lag time, just now. But you knew that.

Szenippet: Every new day requires an end to the day before, but sometimes it's so seamless we never notice.

■ ■ ■

Goal Post
A Sixty-Word SZEN Story:

The mediator became extremely irritated and when he lunged at me across the table, it collapsed beneath his weight and the once beautiful marble slab broke into pieces. He then picked up a piece of the jagged tabletop and holding it like a knife, first wildly swiped at me and then raised it as he charged forward. End of negotiations.

And more...
Ever have a meeting where it seems like nothing gets accomplished? Sometimes there are times when somehow, the objectives are not communicated or the people that have the power to act never show and the wheels of progress spin and never gain traction. Without a clear purpose or goal it's difficult, if not impossible, to have a positive outcome. Goals

set expectations and determine success. And without a goal, whatever happens happens.

Goals are subsets to our vision and are easy to set once we know the ultimate destination. They provide the markers and milestones we need along the way to determine if we're staying on the right course. It could be a degree earned, a career chosen, a language to learn or whatever we need and can be short baby steps or huge leaps of faith. And as we progress, we can then check them off of our list as we pursue our destiny in the making. Reaching a goal is good and missing a goal is an outcome to be learned from.

If we don't examine our goals or our vision from time to time we could find ourselves going through the motions – what looks like activity and positive energy – which really is a mask. In this state we're not measuring progress, but ticks on the clock. Days run into days and eventually the routine becomes the goal. Disrupting the routine, even if it takes an altercation with an agitated mediator, can serve as a wake up call for a new course. It did for me.

Szenippet: Achievement is not only about reaching the goal; it's about setting the right goal to reach. We'll know we've set the right one when we can't wait to get there.

■ ■ ■

Letting Go of Expectations
The great thing about having a hopeful heart is that we can see the potential in anything we choose. We get to pick what we want to believe and what we choose to have faith in. We especially get to hold on to even the slightest of chances, as

if the results we seek were imminent. As long as an idea or dream or potential "deal" has even a flicker of life, we have the power to hold onto its possibilities.

Waiting for an approval or even a response to a proposal, be it business or personal, can weigh heavily on us until we can resolve an outcome. Sometimes things that we have failed to achieve linger in our psyche like a nagging allergy that clogs our mind and limits our clarity. We may know that what we seek may not happen, but until we admit it, we enjoy the thought that there is still a chance.

If we have too many ongoing possibilities to hold onto, it's important that we rank them and let go of the least likely scenarios. The mere act of letting go will free some mind space and simultaneously open the door for some new options. In many cases, the releasing or letting go of the need for a predetermined outcome for a situation is exactly what's needed to bring it closer to reality.

When we lighten our load and transcend the worry state, we begin to see that we cannot manipulate events and people just by wishing for things to go our way.

When we take the pressure off of ourselves from trying to control how we want *everything* to happen, we turn off the worry button. That simple act opens a new flow of positive imagination - A place where new dreams can form and where the possibilities are truly endless.

Szenippet: Dreams don't die; they only leave to make room for what has yet to be dreamed.

Szenippet: Making a wish is the first step in having it come true.

Szenippet: Selective memory is our best weapon in fighting failure.

■ ■ ■

About The Author

Gary Szenderski is an author, speaker, teacher and branding specialist, internationally acclaimed as an expert on the subject. He specializes in helping people and organizations to navigate change, and frequently speaks and writes on the topic of emerging brands, personal branding and companies in transition. Gary is an award-winning writer, author of the Book of Szen, often quoted marketing expert, and recipient of the Distinguished Instructor Award from the University of California in Irvine where he teaches branding. He resides in Southern California and welcomes your comments. Email him at gary@bookofszen.com.

For new stories and information visit www.szenzone.com